I Will Fear No Evil

A MISSIONARY'S FAITH JOURNEY THROUGH FEAR, ANXIETY, DEPRESSION, AND TRAUMA

KAREN BETTISON

BLOOMIN' PEN PUBLISHING
BELLFLOWER, MO, USA

Paperback — ISBN: 979-8-9888520-3-2

E-Book — ISBN: 979-8-9888520-2-5

Library of Congress Control Number: 2024904468

Cover design by: Annette Zacho

Printed in the United States of America

Contents

FOREWORD

I have known Karen for three decades—as both a friend and co-worker. On my first nerve-wracking day in Africa, April 1, 1994, she saved my bacon. Rebecca and I walked slowly through the chaotic airport, eyes darting around, taking in all the confusion as sweat rolled down the backs of my legs from the incredible humidity. I felt over-whelmed by the newness of every sight, sound, and smell. We must have looked completely lost and extremely vulnerable. I had never seen any place like this before.

The airport applied very little investment toward security back then. It seemed to me that the police allowed random people to just waltz in off the street all the way back to where we were collecting our luggage. The whole scene felt more like an open market than a secure airport. So much has changed since then! As I picked up my luggage and rolled it toward the small army of blue-uniformed customs agents milling around by the door, I saw that they were surrounded by a thick throng of travelers somehow passing through. I quickly realized I could be in trouble as they began brusquely pointing and ordering me to plop down my trunks on their counters and open everything up for inspection.

As I nervously mustered my courage to explain myself, suddenly Karen swept onto the scene like an irresistible force of nature. Instantly, she was pushing upstream through the current of people exiting the airport with her arms waving in the air as she yelled Mission Protestante! Swiftly racing about and exclaiming unknown pronouncements in one of the local languages, Karen tipped the metaphorical balance in our favor with the sheer force of her energy.

Unexpectedly every blue uniformed arm began waving us through without inspection. The crowds parted like the Red Sea. Stunned, Rebecca and I staggered after Karen, pushing carts full of luggage without even saying a word of greeting to her. We ambled out into the intense radiation of the African sun under Karen's formidable guidance and protection as she forcefully defended us from all the suspicious characters trying to snatch our luggage as a ruse to make us pay them for carrying it. Whoosh, before I knew it, she was whisking us away in a vehicle, and suddenly sanity descended upon us. Karen toured us around, showing us how to get around in the village and city. She took us places no one should have gone. Her courage was limitless. She looked, in my eyes, like an unshakable warrior.

But now, reading this book, I realize that so much more was going on beneath the surface in Karen's mind. Even while she took on incredible challenges with great bravery, behind the closed doors of her heart, she was dealing with the trauma of it all. This book reveals the deeper thoughts of a great servant of God. She looked on the surface like the kind of person you only read about in missionary biographies. But now, she has taken the trouble to help us understand that God uses regular people to accomplish such feats. She wasn't a person of great courage. She was a person who let God *give* her great courage when she needed it. In this book, she reveals the struggles and anxieties she encountered and how God helped her overcome.

I'm grateful to God that she didn't let fear win out and that she let God take her on this amazing journey. I'm grateful to Karen for helping me and my wife adjust to West Africa. She walked us through that chaos and showed us the ropes. We lived in her house for a while in the village. She was unbelievably fearless in those early years, perhaps to an unhealthy degree. Then later, as the crises and struggles of life kept piling on top of one another, I remember how she came to be more sensitive to danger. I remember the trauma of Jim and Karen's departure, and how we all returned to the States with varying degrees of wounds afflicting us from the traumatic experiences we all had in West Africa. It's cathartic to read her story in detail now.

Most people could never write a book like this one because they haven't taken the pains to journal consistently enough over the years to keep a written record to guide their recollections. Wouldn't it be nice to be able to look back on life and see from hindsight the meaning and impact of what happened? In Karen's case, she has a unique story of work in West Africa on a Bible translation project. Those of us who read her story won't be able to keep from marveling at how well-preserved the important details are and how impactful the spiritual experiences are.

Aspects of the story will resonate with anyone who reads it. We have all had experiences like these. But those of us who have traveled overseas and lived as servants of God in difficult places will especially see in this story elements of our own.

Karen has written not only what happened but how it impacted her as a person. This book opens an intimate window into her story and how God used her experiences, joyful as well as painful, to shape her as a person.

If you read with insight, you just might encounter in Karen's story some of the same influences that shaped your story too. When she writes about how anxieties crept into her life, it may well surface memories in your own life too. When she recounts her story with vulnerability and authenticity, you just might find yourself reflecting suddenly on your own similar experiences, taking you on a similar introspective journey along with her.

May the Lord use this writing to minister to many.

Greg Pruett; President

Pioneer Bible Translators

ACKNOWLEDGEMENTS

The inspiration to write this book came from many friends who were willing to listen to parts of my story and encouraged me to put it into writing. I am grateful to all who walked with me through this, had faith in me, and gave me the courage to do this project.

I am extremely grateful to all those who helped proofread and edit parts or all of this book: my husband, Jim; my mom, Cathi; my daughter, Katie; my friend and colleague, Tina Ganong; and many others mentioned by name in this book.

I am also grateful to the many anonymous missionaries who opened up and allowed themselves to be vulnerable, sharing the hardships of their own journey to help shed light on the widespread struggles missionaries face on the field.

I am indebted to my counselors, Ken Wadum and Alan Lee, who helped me process my trauma.

I am thankful to my colleagues who served God faithfully alongside me during my years in Africa, and who offered their friendship and encouragement along the way.

I am thankful to my "African sister," Annette Zacho, who designed the cover and understands all too well the "beauty and turmoil" of Africa, as she put it.

I thank my parents, who raised me to know the Lord and gave me a foundation of faith, especially my mother, who has always been there to listen. She kept all my correspondence over the years, making recounting many details of my story possible.

I can't say enough how thankful I am for my children, who have graciously put up with me and loved me during the hardest times. I am so grateful for my husband, Jim, who has stood by me through thick and thin, and has been a rock of support for the past 28 years and counting.

Most of all, I'm thankful to Yahweh, Creator of heaven and earth. He loved you and me so much that he came in the form of a man, Jesus, to die for us, giving us real hope in this fallen world. He walks with me and provides for me through the darkest of times. Without him, I would have lost hope long ago.

INTRODUCTION

M emories are powerful things. It's easy to remember good times and forget bad times. Some memories we choose to forget; we leave them hidden deep in the recesses of our subconscious mind. Others are seared into our minds. We cannot ignore them; they haunt us when we least expect it. As we age, we either find it harder to remember details about experiences, or we subconsciously choose to block them out, and their value is lost to us.

From an early age, I kept a diary. My diaries began simply, recording a child's thoughts of wonder at this world, crushes, relationships, and other significant events at the time. They gradually became conversations with God, reflections on spiritual truths I learned, and an account of my journey. When I left home for college and eventually overseas, my family saved letters that gave an account of events as they unfolded. Years later, carefully preserved and stored in boxes, these diaries, journals, and letters became powerful aids to my fading memory of the journey's events, details, and emotions. They also testified to God's faithful care through every step.

I have since learned the power of self-reflection as a means of personal growth. Counselors rely on self-reflection exercises to bring healing to their clients, and higher education employs self-reflection as an academic tool to promote advanced learning. Through self-reflection, one often gains a deeper understanding of oneself, finds meaning and purpose, recognizes strengths and weaknesses, and identifies emerging themes.

Journaling becomes a form of therapy. Re-reading the memories of long ago and seeing the lessons I learned but quickly forgot has been the most beneficial.

Several themes became apparent as I reflected on the events of my life through these journal readings. One was feelings of rejection and inadequacy. Looking back, I realize how many of my decisions, life choices, and my developing self-identity were shaped by events in which I perceived rejection.

Fear and its counterpart anxiety also emerged as central themes. I have always struggled with these emotions. Sometimes I'd gained victory over them, only to succumb again to their grip. And I am not alone. According to Psychology Today, anxiety has become a worldwide epidemic, with the United States in the lead.[1] People of this generation are more likely to report poor mental health than those of the preceding generation.[2]

How is this possible in a society with such technological advances? We live in the lap of luxury, not in poverty like the world's majority population. The United States is not at war like many nations. Christians are not persecuted in the US in the same manner they are in other countries. Yet the struggle to find peace and contentment is somehow out of reach. Societal changes, social media, and conflicting views of science and truth add to the confusion, causing young people to take desperate measures to find meaning, identity, and purpose.

The fact that fear and anxiety are endemic to human experience shouldn't surprise us. In her study "The Epic of Eden," Dr. Sandra Richter suggests that we see the birth of anxiety at the heart of the Curse, as recounted in Genesis 3:17-19, where God tells Adam that through painful toil he will eat from the ground, and by the sweat of his brow he will eat his food. Anxiety has plagued humanity ever since.[3] Danger in this life is real. Our safety, financial stability, and sometimes even our lives are threatened. We are all caught up in a race to survive in a world where death is the final chapter. Even our bodies and minds are innately wired for a "fight or flight" response, no matter how well we learn to master it.

Navigating fear, understanding the whys of the universe, and finding purpose and meaning in this life are the private mission of every member of humanity. How does one break free from the talons of fear? Is there any hope? God has shown us a way: the redemptive plan he set in motion in Eden would find its fulfillment in Christ on the cross. God gives eternal hope to those who trust and follow him. Finding freedom from fear and depression has been my quest as I have endeavored to help myself and others walk through that valley.

In my writing, I do not attempt to recount every life event from my memories or journaling, just the ones which significantly impacted my journey, either positively or negatively. Every choice we make and every experience we have can be significant. The mystery of God's sovereignty and our freedom of choice play out as we journey through life. I believe that God shapes us through our circumstances, events, and the people around us. He works with our interests, abilities, and the unique person he has made us to be, gently wooing us to become part of his bigger story. Yet God allows us to follow our own path, sometimes righting our course at various steps along the way, and sometimes allowing us to reject him completely. God gives us the freedom to explore various scenarios, and we have the choice to learn from each experience. He desires to teach us the great mysteries of who he is and his larger view of things. He knows that we, as part of this fallen, sin-cursed earth, are broken and desperately in need of him. We need God to draw us back and restore our intimate relationship with him.

Sometimes the circumstances God allows us to endure seem harsh and unloving from our self-centered perspective and our wounded state. Yet he remains sovereign and in control. He knows how the story ends and how he desires it to play out. We can't always understand his higher ways in this life, but someday, standing in eternity, everything will become clear. God doesn't expect us to always figure everything out. I certainly do not understand many things from my own life. But our Sovereign does ask us to trust him and his perfect plan. Accepting his plan is at the heart of faith.

So, why did I write this book? As I have shared bits and pieces of my journey with others over the years, many have asked me repeatedly to put my story into writing. In the search to find meaning in my pain, writing this has helped me to sift through the pieces, see the bigger picture, and has brought clarity and meaning to my journey. Even the hidden, most painful parts. Writing them forced me to relive some very difficult moments, often triggering me with some of the same "fight or flight" responses as if I were living them all over again. I have mixed emotions about sharing this part of my story, especially fear. I worry about exposing my emotions, weaknesses, and vulnerable moments for everyone to see and scrutinize. I can only hope that God would use it for his greater glory.

My story is just one story among many. I hope it will shed light on some of the common stressful and traumatic experiences of international workers and the negative consequences these can have on mental health. I pray that in reading my story, they will know that they are not alone. As my dear friend Tina once pointed out, we are normal humans and are not immune to the negative consequences of our environments just because we serve God. Nor will healing come instantly for everyone. Some scars we will carry for a lifetime, apart from divine intervention. We may never completely heal this side of heaven. This holds true for anyone who lives on this planet. Yet there is hope.

Trying to find purpose and meaning in all the difficulties of life often seems out of reach. But even in spite of my inability to always see the "why" of what happened to me, I am sure of one thing: God walked through it with me, cultivated my faith, and ultimately drew me to lean on him more, which is, in my view, the only reason I'm still here. I pray that by walking through my journey, you will discover how God has been ever-present in your journey as well – how he is calling you back to him through your unique circumstances and desires an intimate relationship with you. I pray that the lessons I've learned as I have struggled to overcome my fears and anxiety will help others imprisoned in the grip of the unavoidable symptoms of the Curse to find hope and freedom.

(Names of some places and individuals in this story have been excluded or have been changed for security reasons.)

Chapter One

BEGINNINGS OF FEAR

A s is often the case, the seeds of fear can take root in early childhood. My childhood was overall a happy one, as best as I can remember; I was born in Southern California, the daughter of two parents in ministry who loved me and provided for me. My parents had spent time serving as missionaries in Barbados before I was born. In my earliest years, my father pastored a church. My brother was two and a half years older than I was. There was no abuse or neglect in my family.

When I was around two, my father left the ministry and even left our family for several months, faking his own death. I was too young to understand my father's pain and struggle, how it influenced his actions, or the anguish it must have caused my mother. My brother and I were seemingly unscathed. Our family uprooted and moved to Arizona, and my father returned to us shortly thereafter. My mother graciously welcomed him back, no questions asked.

My first memory of fear was before the age of three, when, while stopped at a rest area in Texas, I let go of my mother's hand to dart across the road. Between the oncoming car stopping abruptly and my mother grabbing me, I avoided a near-fatal accident. This traumatic experience was etched into my mind.

Our family moved back to Illinois when I was three years old. I have many fond memories of childhood: chasing fireflies, romping in the woods with neighborhood kids, attending summer camp, winning 2nd place in the state science fair, and my love for animals, music, ice skating, and art.

There were some fearful memories as well: the strange drunk man who came into our house in the middle of the night when our father was away; getting lost for a day at Disneyland; a friend of my parents injured in a terrible motorcycle accident, leaving him severely brain damaged; another family friend suffering from an aneurysm, causing him to become mentally disabled; and boys in the neighborhood engaging in bloody fistfights. I remember my brother building a clubhouse with a secret hideout dug out underneath it "in case any bad guys should come."

Early memories of shame also are etched in my mind. Once around the age of five, while playing with some boys, I thought it would be empowering to throw a rock at one of them. I hit him on the head and quickly knew what I did was wrong. Full of shame, I ran into the house and hid in the clothes hamper, thinking I could somehow shut out the world and escape the consequences I feared. But my mother quickly found me and made me fess up to what I had done. I had to tell the boy, "Sorry," and confess my actions to both our mothers.

On another occasion, I was around eight years old on a family trip to visit relatives in Virginia. I snuck out of the house early one morning to visit the pony in their pasture. After climbing under the wooden fence, the pony saw me and began trotting in my direction, probably hoping for a sweet handout. I panicked, turned, and ran in the other direction. I tripped on a dry well cover as I ran and fell unconscious. When I came to, I didn't know where I was. It took me a while to realize what had happened. What's worse, I discovered that I was soaking wet. At first, I thought it was blood and panicked; then I realized I had wet myself. I was so embarrassed and ashamed and wanted to hide the fact I had even been in the horse pen in the first place. But I needed to change my clothes, which meant telling my mother. I went to her sobbing and told her what had happened, hoping she would feel sorry for me since I was hurt. Instead, she became upset with me. I felt public shame in front of all the relatives because of my poor judgment.

Another time I remember trying to go "no-handed" on my bike. I was going fast and closed my eyes for a brief moment, feeling the cool evening breeze blow against my face. Suddenly, I hit a telephone pole head-on and crashed. The next thing I knew, I woke up dazed in the middle of the street. My skinned arms and legs were oozing blood. Apparently, I had passed out. I felt ashamed. This time, I did not tell my mom what happened, fearing her wrath for acting so foolishly. I covered my wounds with Band-Aids and wore long sleeves to hide the abrasions.

No one debriefed trauma back then. I got the idea in my head that traumatic events were to be minimized, hidden, and brushed off, so I stuffed my emotions inside. I often associated anxiety and trauma with public shame, especially when it resulted from my own poor choices. Admitting I did something wrong brought scorn instead of sympathy. I came to fear that scorn and shame so much that I second-guessed myself and even tormented myself with doubts about my goodness and worth when traumatic things happened.

As a young child, I gained a reputation for being "shy." This was most evident when I was asked to be in front of crowds. I dreaded being upfront or the center of attention. During our church's Christmas play when I was six, we all had a role to learn and act out or a song to sing. However, when it was time to perform on stage in front of the congregation, I froze. I refused to go on with everyone else. All I could see were the eyes of the crowd bearing down on me. No amount of coercion could make me get on that stage. My behavior bordered on a tantrum. I'm sure the play directors let me have my way to avoid making a scene or humiliating me publicly. They allowed me to sit in the front row and watch the play instead.

Later, when my mother enrolled me in piano lessons, I was required to perform in my first recital. My piano teacher held recitals at a real concert hall on a big stage with bright spotlights and, you guessed it, crowds!

At that first recital, I remember standing backstage waiting for my turn. Peering through the curtain, I saw the pianist in front of me, dwarfed by an enormous grand piano in the center of the stage. What seemed like hundreds of people were sitting in the audience, focusing their full attention on the performer. Then the realization hit me: I was next! I could feel fear rising inside of me. What if I messed up? What if they didn't like me? I couldn't stand the thought of being the object of all those people's scrutiny. I had a full-blown case of stage fright and insisted I could not play. I remember a woman standing there with me, maybe my mother or a helper. She kept urging me to go out on stage. But I froze and wouldn't budge. For the second time in my life, the adults in the room avoided a spectacle by skipping me and proceeding with the next performer. I decided to give up rather than face my fears.

The next time there was a piano recital, I pretended to be sick so I wouldn't have to go. I genuinely felt sick from anxiety. From that point on, my mother just gave up trying to make me perform. She resigned herself to the fact that I was just "shy."

In the summer when I was eight years old, tragedy struck my family. We had just returned from a family vacation. My father was away on an overnight freelance trucking job. Early the next morning on July 6th, two of my father's best friends, John and Jerry, came to the door. I looked out the window and saw them. "Mom! The preacher and Jerry are here," I announced. My mom's countenance quickly changed. "Oh no, not again!" she said. I didn't understand what she meant. But when they came into the house, it soon became clear that our lives would never be the same again. On his way back home at 6 a.m., my father was killed in an accident. The authorities thought that he had fallen asleep at the wheel.

Immediately my mother called the neighbors, who agreed to take care of us while she dealt with the investigation into his death and made funeral arrangements. Hoping to get our minds off the tragedy, the neighbors took us to a carnival in the neighborhood. I remember the surreal feeling of eating cotton candy, trying to feel "normal," but knowing deep inside nothing was normal. We stayed with friends from the church for several days until the funeral. I don't remember being allowed to see my father up close at the funeral, and for years afterward, I dreamt he was still alive and would mysteriously reappear someday. Then everything would be normal again.

We watched as Dad's casket was lowered into the ground at the grave site. My grandmother pointed out that he was being buried next to a close friend's child, as the child's parents had requested. The boy had died after his brother accidentally stabbed him with a barbecue skewer while pretending to sword fight. I shivered, thinking how it must feel to kill someone by accident, let alone your own brother. I imagined the boy would never get over his feelings of guilt.

In the days that followed, conversations with my mom and our pastor about my dad's death led me to give my life to Christ and be baptized. The realization that God loved me as a father took on special meaning as he took the place of my earthly father. With my new-found faith, I felt joy and peace inside.

I was one of the smart girls in class and an overachiever, but my shyness caused me to be introverted. I would often bond with my teachers, and I developed a strong sense of personal accomplishment in my talents and academic achievement. However, I always felt the other girls despised me for my achievements. I was frequently the last one picked on teams at school and sometimes bullied. I struggled with feelings of rejection, low self-worth, and inadequacy. In many ways, this made me stronger on my own, more independent, and more prone to lean into God for strength. In other ways, I often felt wounded and was prone to depression.

Despite feeling alienated from some of the girls at church and school, I eventually did develop close friendships as I got older through Girl Scouts and church camp. I remember girls at camp screaming in the night when the camp cat snuck into the cabin, or the ripples of panic as a rogue bee buzzed around the campfire, stinging unsuspecting campers because his nest had been disturbed. But even in those moments, there was a sense that nothing seemed too ominous within the safe circle of friends and counselors. At the end of the day, we all somehow felt all would be well. The relationships built moved me further and further out of my social anxiety. I learned to feel more accepted and part of something bigger than myself and began to feel safety in groups.

When I was 11, while attending a Christian camp, I listened to a guest missionary who had served in the Congo. After hearing him speak, I felt a fire rise inside me, a longing to be a part of something so adventurous and pleasing to God as serving on the mission field. I knew then that I wanted to become a missionary and was particularly intrigued by Africa.

Over the next few years, as I began high school, I entertained other career pathways, such as art or zoology. For two years, I worked as a zoo volunteer and was given a lot of responsibility. At one point, I was even featured in an article in the local newspaper. Speaking about animals and my experiences there helped me to slowly overcome my fear of speaking in front of crowds.

One day, my mother was boasting about my accomplishments at the zoo to one of her church friends. The woman replied, "Too bad she doesn't care about people as much as she cares about animals." That statement cut me to the core, and I realized I had set aside my interest in becoming a missionary. I'm sure the woman probably never realized the impact her words had on me and how it would change the course of my life.

During the summer of 1980, the tugging at my heart to serve as a missionary became even stronger when, again, several missionaries spoke at our church and at camp, sharing their work in India and Africa. I began to feel God had destined me for the mission field, particularly Africa. My dream of a career with animals began to fade.

When I was 15, my family moved to the St. Louis area. We joined a Christian church where I grew spiritually in a thriving youth group. In time, I bonded with the kids in the youth group and began growing more spiritually. A whole world opened to me of living the Christian life the way God wanted me to.

There was no end to the exciting things the youth group did: attending city-wide youth outings, Bible studies in each other's homes, youth choir, summer camp, overnight lock-ins, and more. Almost everyone was in the youth choir, so I joined to be a part of the group. When it was time to perform in front of the church, I found that I enjoyed it as long as I was in a group.

Because my mother was on staff at a local Christian college, I spent a lot of time hanging around the campus and consequently got to know many students. Many of them were preparing to serve as missionaries. As time passed, I became less concerned about high school and set my sites on college, determined to attend there as soon as possible. I took summer classes so that I could graduate early.

In the fall of 1982, my senior year in high school, I took an honors art course called the Senior Art Portfolio, in which I spent the whole afternoon every day in intensive art classes. I honed my skills in various media like drawing, paper making, and clay. Our goal was to put together art pieces representing our diverse artistic talent for presentation in a portfolio exhibit at the end of the semester. Talent scouts from all the major art schools in the country were invited. I had the special attention of my teachers who felt I could go far with an art career. They told me I could ask any talent scout for a scholarship the evening of the exhibit, and

I would have it. For a brief moment, I would imagine an art career. But deep down, I knew it wasn't for me. I sensed that God had something more in store for me, even though it went against what all my high school counselors suggested.

On the night of the exhibit, my thoughts were confirmed when I met the talent scouts. I knew that I did not belong in their world. When my teachers asked me what I had decided, I told them I had already planned to graduate high school early and attend a Bible college in the spring.

After the exhibit was over, my mother came to take me home. As we started to leave, I realized I had forgotten something in the school, so I went back inside. Before I turned the corner into the exhibit hall, I heard my two teachers talking. They were telling each other how I was wasting my life going to a Bible college and throwing away a huge opportunity. I walked up to them just as they were saying this. They stopped talking, looking at me silently and ashamedly. The feeling of shame at being the object of someone's gossip was quickly overcome by my disappointment in them, which showed on my face. I said nothing, picked up my things, and walked away. And just like that, my choice determined my future. I knew I was making the right decision for myself.

At the age of 17, I began classes at Bible College. I auditioned for a traveling camp team on a dare and was accepted. Traveling with the team turned out to be a very positive experience. I made many lasting friendships, which helped me gain more confidence singing, speaking in public, and sharing my testimony.

During the following school year, my interest in overseas missions intensified. I considered medical mission work as a specialty, following my passion for science and biology. I joined the campus missions group and began taking classes in missionary life and work. Everything I learned was new, exciting, and challenging. I felt compelled more and more to give my life in missionary service as I learned of the many thousands of unreached people groups, each with its unique language and culture.

I learned of missionaries like Jim Elliot and Nate Saint, who lost their lives to the Auca Indians in Ecuador. My mother gave me my father's copy of Elisabeth Elliot's book *Through Gates of Splendor,*[1] in which my dad had made his own personal notes. I treasured this book and considered it a privilege to follow in my dad's footsteps. Hearing how God's kingdom was advanced through the heroic bravery of missionaries inspired me. As one missionary spoke in chapel one day, his words gave me courage. I heard him say that the mission field seemed like a scary place to some, but there was no safer place than in the center of God's will. I clung to this idea, believing God protected those who followed him.

Chapter Two

SURRENDER

My first year of college was life-changing in so many ways. I spent hours in prayer and spiritual development. I prayed every day for God's guidance and direction for a field where I could serve.

In my third semester, however, I had a major emotional setback. I experienced betrayal from a friend that set my emotions reeling, resulting in my first real bout of depression. The feelings of rejection and betrayal lingered and played a role in my emotional state. By the end of the spring semester of 1984, my newfound ambitions for serving as an overseas missionary came to a standstill. I became increasingly discouraged and depressed about my future. Disillusionment set in, and I considered changing schools and majors. I prayed desperately for God to show me his will for my life and the path I should take.

Then, unexpectedly, I was invited by my uncle, Rondal, to travel with him and his daughter, Andria, to Papua New Guinea. Papua New Guinea, a large island nation off the northern coast of Australia, is home to over 800 indigenous peoples, each with their own language. Rondal was serving with a new organization, Pioneer Bible Translators, which had started several Bible translation projects there. A spark of hope returned. It didn't take me long to realize I had to try and make this happen. My energy suddenly took a new direction. I would have to get a passport and visa, raise the money, and buy plane tickets all in the next six weeks. For the first time, I had a solid plan, even if it was short-term, and it gave me a renewed passion and momentum. Again, another crossroad moment in time unfolded, and the direction of my future changed.

In the following weeks, I prayed, gathered resources, and saved money. I sold many of my personal belongings and asked friends at church for financial help. However, as I made plans to go to Papua New Guinea, my mind kept drifting to thoughts of the hot climate and the many diseases there. I had heard stories of people with leprosy and missionaries dying from malaria and other tropical diseases. What if I got some tropical disease and died in the rainforest before I could reach help?

What's worse, not long ago, the people of this land were head-hunters. I imagined meeting an entourage of grass-skirt-clad warriors with bone-pierced noses and spears in hand. Would they be the ones to meet me at the airport? Thoughts about what happened to the missionaries in Ecuador came to mind. The reality of it all began to sink in, and the fears slowly consumed my thoughts. My imagination worked overtime, conjuring up more things to worry about. No sooner than the fear of disease or headhunters finally subsided, the idea of dying in a plane crash would come to mind.

Eventually, I decided that it all boiled down to surrender. I would have to let go of my fear and give in to God's peace. I had to accept that the worst-case scenario could happen, and if it did, I would have to trust that God held me. Besides, I reminded myself of what I had heard that missionary say in chapel: that there was no safer place than in the center of God's will. I read the words of King David in Psalm 23, which said,

> *Even though I walk*
> *through the darkest valley,*
> *I will fear no evil,*
> *for you are with me;*
> *Your rod and your staff,*
> *they comfort me.*[1]

I reasoned that if God wanted me to go, then I would have to believe he would protect me as a shepherd protected his sheep with his rod and staff from harm along the way, and therefore I had nothing to fear. Six weeks later, passport, visa, and tickets in hand, I was on my way.

As we entered the airport of Port Moresby, the capital of Papua New Guinea, we came through a thick mist with the moon shining down. Once we landed, I was quite relieved that we were greeted by uniformed airport personnel instead of headhunters. We arrived at our guest hostel late and got to bed around 1:30 a.m. I had a hard time sleeping. My head was spinning from the jetlag and the change in altitude, and my stomach was churning. I drifted in and out of sleep, dragged in by fatigue and awakened periodically by various night sounds outside my window: crunching, squealing, barking, scratching, gnawing, and buzzing noises, all choreographed on top of a constant hum of crickets.

When we woke at 5:30, we had less than an hour to be at the airport for our connecting flight to Madang in the northern part of the country. After navigating the usual traffic jam outside the small terminal and the chaos inside the airport, we boarded our plane just in time. As we flew over the mountain range that bisects the country, I took in the breathtaking view until we entered a cloud front that dumped heavy torrents of rain on the town of Lae below, where we landed briefly.

As we arrived in Madang, dozens of children peered through the airport's screened windows waiting to see who would get off the plane. Finally, our PBT missionary colleagues, Eunice and Mike, met us. They blessed us with warm hospitality and fellowship for several days as they introduced us to their work and helped us begin learning some of the local trade language, Tok Pisin, and navigating the local customs.

After several days, we departed from Madang on a twin-engine plane to the village of Garati in the Madang Province, where a PBT couple, David and Sharran, and their two children, lived and worked among the

Kire people. We bonded quickly with their family as they welcomed us warmly and shared their insights into the language and culture of the Kire people.

That week, we took walks in the village every day. The Kire people greeted us enthusiastically. We observed them preparing their meals from abundant natural jungle foods and cultivated gardens. They prepared yams, bananas, tobacco, sugar cane, the glue-like dish "sak-sak" made from the starch of the Sago palm tree, cooked greens, coconuts, and grilled bandicoot (a rodent-like marsupial). We enjoyed the refreshing green coconut milk, feasting on raw sugar cane, and drinking the cool water carried in bamboo reeds.

The young girls we met laughed with each other as we attempted to speak their language. Yet they seemed to communicate that they appreciated our efforts. The village children teased us as they laughed shyly to each other at our strange behavior. We attended Bible studies and nights of singing, praying, and talking with village members. We traveled down the river in motorized dugout canoes to visit nearby villages. It didn't take me long to feel at ease and unafraid in this environment.

One evening we walked down to the village for a prayer meeting. The night sky was clear and amazingly brilliant as the stars pierced the blackness, uninhibited by smog or light. A falling star flashed across the night sky overhead, the biggest, brightest one I had ever seen. The Southern Cross constellation, which I had never seen before from my previous vantage point in the northern hemisphere, was now visible.

One single lamp lit up the area as we sat around the courtyard. The villagers sang mostly familiar tunes, but in the Tok Pisin language, which I found easy to learn. They started with light-hearted songs, then gradually moved on to more serious songs, which everyone sang with increased energy and enthusiasm. It was indeed an uplifting experience. Though culturally worlds apart, I felt at one with these people as we all worshipped together the one true God.

It had turned dark by the time David and Sharran's son, John, led us back to the house. No one had thought to bring a flashlight. I had never walked in total darkness before and was concerned that we might lose our way, or worse, step on a snake or something equally menacing. Unconcerned, John knew the path by heart and chatted away as we followed the sound of his voice and footsteps. We walked blindly in the dark, trusting our guide's voice. The analogy to my own unknown journey did not escape me. God was asking me to trust him and follow his voice down an unseen path.

One day I was visiting some village women and attempting to practice language learning when a woman held out her newborn baby for me to hold. My heart melted as I looked into the face of this tiny, delicate child with beautiful features and large, black eyes that glowed back with so much expression. I was captivated. After that, the women seemed more comfortable around me. I fell in love with these people and their home.

Sharran shared my sentiment and said she felt more at home there after seven years than anywhere else she had been. The people in Garati had taught her to slow down, enjoy God, nature, and life in general, and find real peace. In my heart, I knew God was showing me this as well.

One afternoon, I was invited to sit in on a Bible translation session with Rondal, David, and three men who were Kire speakers who also spoke a good amount of English. As they discussed the particulars of a specific passage of Scripture, I listened intently to the discussion. At one point, David turned to me and asked, "Karen, what do you think?" Surprised they would invite me into their discussion, I offered my opinion. At that moment, one of the Kire co-translators looked at me and said, "You would make a good Bible translator."

The man's statement stuck with me. Could I do this? Someone actually had confidence that I could. The thought of doing Bible translation had never occurred to me.

I learned from my uncle that he, Janice, my father, and several of their friends who all attended Bible college together years ago had dreamed of someday starting a mission organization together. My father was dead. But now, all the other members of the group were, in one way or another, involved in the ministry of PBT. Was I a missing piece of the puzzle? Was God somehow orchestrating events so I could be a part of my father's prayer-filled dream? Ironically, my brother decided to join PBT and had already started the training process that summer. Should I do the same? I began entertaining the idea.

After a week in Garati, we traveled by plane to Samban village, where David's brother, John, and wife, Bonita, translated the Bible for the people who spoke the Ap Ma language. This village was in the middle of a mosquito-infested swamp. Since it was now dry season, the area was only experiencing a moderate quantity of mosquitos.

They teamed me up with a young, local girl my age named Juliana to start learning the Ap Ma language and culture in yet another setting. Over the next two weeks, I spent significant time with Juliana and her family and neighbors. They taught me to fish by hand in the river, wash sago pulp, prepare "sak-sak," weave baskets, and do many other daily survival tasks while I attempted to learn as much of the language as I could. In the evenings, covered with dirt, sweat, and copious mosquito bites, I would heat water on the stove and take a "bucket shower."

Despite the heat and the incessant itching of the hundreds of bites on my legs, I enjoyed my time there immensely. Once again, I quickly developed a bond with John and Bonita's family, as well as with Juliana and her family.

One Sunday afternoon, John and Bonita's children and many of their village friends were running in the forest chasing butterflies. Andria and I followed them into the forest to see why they were making such a fuss. As we walked into the shade of the tall forest canopy, the stifling temperature became more bearable without the sun beating down.

Butterflies with the most amazing colors and patterns fluttered by us. It was truly breathtaking. Before long, we joined in the fun, all of us running barefoot on the damp, black mud of the forest floor, laughing so hard our sides ached. That night I sank into bed exhausted yet very content.

While resting in the missionaries' home one afternoon, Bonita was listening to the radio broadcast for the US military living abroad. My mind drifted to the sounds of the announcer describing the opening ceremonies of the Olympics being held a world away in Los Angeles. At that moment, I realized that I had completely forgotten about the outside world. Time seemed to stand still here in the jungle. At times I felt as if I was living in the Stone Age, centuries removed from Western civilization as I knew it. Yet this place, so remote and "backward," held me in its trance. I began to care less and less about the rest of the world with all its trappings.

One day Juliana and several village women took me to the forest to harvest sago palm branches so they could teach me how to make baskets. One woman started the basket for me, her fingers blending the weave with ease and style. Then she handed it to me to let me try it. My fingers stumbled over the twine. As we sat there, the women patiently engaged me in conversation, drilling me on new words and challenging me with more difficult phrases. I was overwhelmed as I stumbled along, trying to keep up.

Nevertheless, I felt a great sense of acceptance as we forged a friendship beyond what words could communicate. I remember feeling perfectly content at that moment – as if I never wanted to be anywhere else. The shy little girl who felt rejected and bullied years ago was now being embraced and entirely accepted by a people a world away.

I felt deeply sad about leaving Samban when the two weeks were up. With black mud deeply embedded in the soles of my feet and my legs covered in hundreds of small bites, the friendships and memories made there left an even more indelible impression on me. I knew that I would miss these people and this country terribly. I also knew I wanted this life.

Chapter Three

UNDAUNTED

In the fall, after returning from Papua New Guinea, I had a new sense of direction and purpose. My experience in PNG allowed me to picture myself in a third-world situation for the first time. Not only did I know that I had what it took, but I also felt as if I were made to live that kind of life.

I was excited about the possibility of being a Bible translator for an unreached people group. But I was torn. I still had the desire to do medical mission work as well. Could I do both? And I was still single. What if I never met someone I wanted to marry who shared my passion? Could I serve as a single woman? I pondered these questions as I continued taking classes at Bible College and began pre-nursing courses at the local community college.

In December of 1984, our college missions group took a trip to Urbana '84. This missions conference occurred every few years, where college students could explore mission careers with hundreds of mission organizations serving worldwide in every capacity. At a main session, I heard Marilyn Laszlo speak about how she, as a single missionary in Papua New Guinea, together with another single lady, translated the Bible into a local language and led a people group to Christ. I felt convinced this was my life's calling. I was also privileged to hear Elisabeth Elliot, the widow of martyred Jim Elliot, speak. These women and others serving overseas became my role models.

I officially began nursing school in fall. To pay for school, I took on various jobs: babysitting, working as an aid in a nursing home, working at a local pet store, and tutoring beginner skating students at a local ice rink. After two years of hard work, I passed my board exams to become a registered nurse.

With an associate degree in nursing and several years of Bible College under my belt, I transferred to a Bible college in Tennessee where I could combine my degrees into one. A local hospital hired me for my first nursing job, and I also became a member-in-training with PBT. A year later, I had a Bachelor's degree in Bible and Nursing. With my degree in hand, I could finally begin training as a Bible translator.

I moved to Dallas, the home of PBT's headquarters, and enrolled in graduate courses in linguistics. Working as a nurse at a local hospital on the weekends helped pay the school bills. I found it providential that my roommate in the dorm, Rose, was a missionary nurse who worked in West Africa and was also training to be a Bible translator. Rose and I got along well and forged a lasting friendship.

The coursework that semester was rigorous. At one point, I began to doubt whether I was doing the "right" thing for my life and whether I had heard God's calling correctly. Discouraging thoughts began creeping into my mind, and depression set in. I struggled with the fact that I still was not married. I prayed every day that God would bring me a godly husband: a soul mate who shared my passion for the lost. Should I really go to the mission field alone?

I became good friends with many young men who shared a desire for ministry among the Bible-less, yet none seemed suitable. I knew many single women had become successful missionaries, but deep inside, I didn't want to be among them. I wanted to go to the mission field married. I had faithfully responded to the call to become a missionary. I had taken action. I had prayed fervently. Why was I still single? Why was I so unhappy? Had I done something wrong, missed a turn, or some direction God had given me? How long would I have to wait for God to answer my prayer? Would God answer my prayer? Like David cried out to God in the book of Psalms, I cried out desperately to God for an answer.

At the time, I sensed that perhaps God was no longer blessing me. I played my failures over and over in my mind, wondering where I had gone wrong. I began to struggle deeply with depression and my identity. At one point, a well-meaning individual blamed my depression on a weak spiritual life, which I found offensive since I spent hours praying daily, journaling, and talking things out with God. However, I could not grasp why I felt this way, so I prayed to God for answers.

Then, like a breath of fresh air, the answer seemed to come. In a moment of vulnerability, I shared how I was feeling with a girl on campus whom I barely knew. Her response was just what I needed, like a whisper of hope from God as I sat on the edge of a huge precipice with no way across. She loaned me a Christian book that said how it is natural for our hearts to ache in this life for something out of reach because we were made for heaven, yet we find ourselves in a sin-cursed world. Our deepest longings often remain unmet, like a missing piece preventing you from completing a puzzle. Only God can truly satisfy those longings, and they might never be met this side of heaven.[1]

For the first time, I finally understood that the dissonance I felt in my life was normal. I was coming to terms with the reality of the curse in which we all find ourselves. My perfect plan was unraveling since the Cinderella complex often leads to disappointment. Perhaps I had made finding a husband an idol in my life. I had to resign myself to the possibility that Prince Charming might never come.

My roommate, herself a single missionary, had long ago concluded that so many single women were on the mission field because the men were disobeying God and not answering the call. This was a sobering idea. I might have to go it alone. I didn't know what else to do but remain faithful, keep praying and hoping, yet continue to move forward and entrust my heart and life to God's hands.

That year, there was a lot of talk about the vast opportunities for Bible Translation and literacy opening throughout West Africa. Independent African governments were eager to implement education programs in national languages, but their employees were ill-equipped to do so. A great need existed for trained field linguists to develop the writing systems of these languages. This presented an opportunity to influence evolving policies. The tug toward Africa from my childhood years reached a new fervor. Great opportunities for single women were opening up in these fields as well.

In early 1989, I learned that a PBT couple, Brent and Ellen, were hoping to open a new field in West Africa. Intrigued, I began discussing with them the possibilities of my working alongside them. Soon, one of my new roommates, Yolanda, and I began planning to visit them in Africa the following spring.

My former roommate, Rose, now back in West Africa herself, had also invited us to visit her. She hoped we could help her evaluate literacy materials for the language group where she worked. So, Yolanda and I made plans to see her in May of 1990 after visiting our PBT colleagues in March and April. The only means of communication, besides expensive long-distance phone calls, was "snail mail." I wrote Rose to tell her of our plans to visit her in May.

In February, however, Yolanda and I received some unexpected, tragic news from Brent and Ellen. Brent, his 11-year-old son, another missionary, and an African pastor were involved in a terrible accident. The other missionary was killed. Their son almost died and was evacuated to Europe for medical treatment. We made plans to visit Rose first to give Brent and Ellen's family time to recuperate. We called the director of Rose's mission who messaged her that we would be coming in the first part of March instead.

Chapter Four

WEST AFRICA

From the late 1800s until the mid-1950s, France colonized much of West Africa, establishing the French language as the language of business, government, and education. By 1960, eight different West African countries had declared their independence from France, establishing their own sovereign nations. Despite this, the French language remains to this day the dominant trade language of these countries.

With barely a few words of French under our belts, Yolanda and I flew to West Africa for the first time on March 1st, 1990. Fear of the unknown gave way to a sense of purpose and adventure as well as hopeful anticipation of realizing a life-long dream. I was confident God would pave the way for us. I waited expectantly to see what opportunities would unfold. I prayed that God would reveal his plan for my future by the end of our six-week trip.

After landing in Bamako, Mali, around 11 p.m., we entered the airport terminal. We made a mad scramble through the arriving crowd to get our passports checked and reclaim our luggage. About a dozen Africans tried to carry our bags, but they left us alone when we kept telling them in broken French that we had no money.

We looked around for Rose, who was supposed to meet us. But she was nowhere to be seen. So, we waited. And waited. Finally, we both became worried as the number of people in the terminal dwindled to very few. Should we take a taxi? If so, where? With no phone numbers, no local money, and no idea how to even make a phone call, we didn't know where we should go, what we should do, or whom we could trust.

Then we noticed about 12 foreigners speaking English, appearing to be seeing someone off, so we approached them. We asked them if they knew Rose. Thankfully one of them did, and they offered to take us to their house until Rose's director could be reached. After a few phone calls were made, we spent the night at the director's house. The next day, we learned Rose had not gotten the message. Thankfully, she could travel down to meet us the following day.

It was the peak of dry season in the Sahel region, a vast band of arid brushland that stretches between the Sahara Desert and the more lush, forested coastal areas of West Africa. We traveled up-country through the sparse vegetation, passing round huts made of red mud bricks. Some huts had grass roofs, while others were covered with tin coated in red, powdery dust. After two days of travel, the paved roads gave way to more dirt and red dust as the terrain became more and more desert-like. The heat was intense and dry.

Finally, we reached the village where Rose worked as a nurse and Bible translator. We drifted off to sleep to the sound of children's voices singing to the rhythm of some unknown instruments off in the distance. Their songs blended with dogs barking and strange insects, birds, and other creatures humming in the cool night air under a clear, moonlit sky.

Rose took us on a village tour on our second day. At one point, we saw several drunk villagers carrying on loudly, taking sips of an alcoholic beverage from several calabash gourds. They signaled us to come over. Rose immediately began conversing with them in the local language, speaking rather forcefully and intently with a tall, boisterous man. Yolanda and I stood there, clueless. Finally, Rose informed us that she had just sold me to the man for six camels and asked me if I agreed. I refused, of course, and everyone got a good laugh out of it.

We spent that week working alongside Rose and her team of African co-translators. We pored over word lists, counting how frequently their letters appeared. Then we devised lessons, using the most frequently used letters first, and helped her team write stories to accompany them. By the end of two weeks, we had helped them develop five primer lessons, a plan for completing the primer series, and a sketch of how a local literacy program should look.

As our time there ended, Yolanda and I gratefully acknowledged how God used us to help the literacy project get underway. Our time in Mali allowed us to do a "trial run" in preparing literacy materials. This encouraged us as we anticipated our departure to meet Brent and Ellen in a neighboring coastal country.

As our plane prepared to land along the West African coast, the view overwhelmed me emotionally. It was breathtaking: a lush, green paradise with mountainous ridges covered with thick, tropical vegetation. I had a strong sense of being "home" and imagined that I would spend my life in this place.

Yolanda and I traveled to the village where Brent, Ellen, and their three children lived and worked. Brent, their two daughters, and Jackie, a nurse, welcomed us warmly. Ellen and their son were still away in Europe, where their son was recovering from the accident.

The new environment supplied abundant food: fish, beef, chicken, eggs, fresh papaya, pineapple, mangos, oranges, bananas, rice, sugar, and cornmeal. But with a lack of refrigeration, Brent's family needed to buy fresh provisions every few days. We learned how they preserved meat and other foods by canning. In addition, we had to filter water and limit our showers to a bucket of hand-pumped well water. We washed dishes by hand and prepared meals from scratch. Everyone in the house pitched in.

Soon we began working with Brent to analyze the local language's sound system and evaluate which letters should be taught first in the primer series. We pushed ourselves to get a lot done in a short amount of time. The intense workweek and the changes in diet, combined with the rigorous daily chores in the intense heat and humidity, all began to take their toll on us. I had trouble sleeping at night as I lay in sticky sweat under a mosquito net with no breeze and often no electricity to run a fan. Lack of sleep and hot, muggy days sapped my energy. My gut churned at night, trying to adjust to the new menu.

In addition to this, the cultural and environmental adjustments wore on me. Brent and Ellen's family lived alongside a large African family's cluster of houses inhabited by an elder of the village, his four wives, and their 25 children. A constant chorus of background noises filled the air: radios blaring, roosters crowing, pots and pans clanging, and women and children bickering.

We took the opportunity to explore life in the village almost daily. I eagerly met people and learned more of their language and culture. However, even simple walks around the village exhausted me under the unrelenting sun with no rain and little breeze. Also, this people group, though very friendly, was a lot louder and more verbally expressive than I was used to. Villagers were often heard arguing loudly with one another.

In addition, Brent and Ellen ran a small medical clinic out of their front room. Jackie, a nurse, had come for a few years to help them treat sometimes 50 patients a day. At times, a constant stream of visitors came to the house. Village children would peek in the windows out of curiosity. Also, hired workers were plastering cement outside the house, preparing it to be painted. The flurry of activity and lack of privacy sometimes overwhelmed me.

After a few weeks, I came down with a sore throat and cough, in addition to the ongoing stomach complaints. I realized I was worn down.

I needed to rest more, take naps, and pace myself to survive the heat and the challenges of this new environment.

Despite the stresses and adjustments of the new culture, the living situation, and the climate, our little team accomplished a lot that first month. We rough-drafted the first eleven primer lessons in a very short time. However, we still had quite a lot of work left to do, so Yolanda and I extended our stay two more months upon Brett and Ellen's invitation to complete the entire series. On one occasion, we met with members of the government linguistic and literacy offices who took a keen interest in our primers and expressed a desire to collaborate.

This opportunity to make meaningful contributions encouraged Yolanda and me to consider returning full-time. Another organization also invited us to assist in developing literacy materials for three other language projects. We knew we couldn't accomplish that goal during this visit. But their invitation confirmed that God was moving and opening a door for us to minister more long-term in West Africa. Unfortunately, Yolanda would not be ready to come for some time. But I was nearly ready, so I considered returning alone to begin the work after gaining better French proficiency.

In addition to the linguistic work, I spent a good amount of time working with Jackie in her front-room clinic. Soon I spent time every day working with a young invalid named Brahiim and his family, teaching them to patiently feed him and nurse him back to health. I also helped tend to numerous burn patients daily.

We periodically traveled to the capital city to buy groceries and other supplies. Policemen and soldiers routinely stopped us at various checkpoints. Many of these encounters could significantly delay our plans for the day, as the officers would often accuse us of some traffic violations of which we were unaware. These officers could be very intimidating. Their voices often reflected a certain degree of posturing, threats, and gravity, indicating we were in a lot of trouble unless, of course, we chose to take care of things the easy way, under the table, so to speak.

These situations would generally cause a lot of stress. However, Jackie had her customary way of dealing with these officers. She had one great thing to her advantage – her age. Older individuals were highly regarded in the culture. Jackie held a special status that younger women did not have, and she used this to her full advantage.

She also knew that the proper way to greet someone was a long, drawn-out process. You would not simply say hello to someone. You had to ask about the person's mother, father, children, brother, spouse, extended family, and the whole village. In fact, the more things you asked about the person and their life, the better. How was their health? How was their work going? Was there any evil in their day?

The first time I was with Jackie, and we got stopped by an officer, she didn't hesitate to venture into the standard greeting ritual as a diversion. She then moved into more critical questions in her broken version of the local language, "Do you have diarrhea? Does your stomach hurt? I have medicine for that!" The man, completely taken aback, started laughing hysterically and summoned one of his fellow officers over to partake in the spectacle. Before long, they were all acting as if they had known Jackie for years and were best friends. Of course, they let Jackie go on her way without any further harassment. Over time, I took my cues from Jackie and others and learned to navigate my way through these situations.

On some occasions, we would take a taxi to town, which was an ordeal in itself. There were always more people waiting for taxis than there were taxis, with people crowding and pushing rather than waiting politely in line. To get a seat, you had to push your way into the seat before anyone else could and hope that your traveling companions also got seats. The whole scenario was reminiscent of children playing a game of musical chairs. Having to be rude or selfish to get anywhere went against all the etiquette I had grown up with. But that was how it was done.

On one occasion, a taxi driver with a small, green, banged-up taxi offered to give us a ride to the market 15 minutes away. The cab resembled a skeleton, with its interior parts stripped bare to make room for more passengers. The remaining upholstery was badly torn. Most of the vehicle had rusted ages ago. The exterior had pieces broken off, and new replacements from various other models tacked on like a patchwork quilt with rusty edges. The driver packed us in like sardines and somehow managed to pick up even more passengers along the way and stuff them in. The engine barely worked. I wondered if we would reach our destination before the whole taxi fell apart.

After the taxi driver stripped the gears several times, trying to start the engine, our vehicle lunged forward, beginning our roller-coaster ride. His car had apparently never seen shock absorbers, so we felt an intimate connection with every bump, jolt, and ripple of the washboard-like road. He raced down the road matter-of-factly, twisting the steering wheel in one direction to avoid one pothole, then jerking it toward smaller holes to avoid the bigger ones. His own body rocked up and down, along with all his passengers. It was shocking yet comical at the same time, and we couldn't help but burst into laughter. He would coast down the hills with the engine off. Then, right before another hill began, he would pop in the clutch, turn the starter, sometimes grinding the gears again, and jolt up the next stretch.

On another occasion, I sat in the front seat of a taxi whose gas tank consisted of a five-gallon plastic jug cut in half, full of fuel, and resting next to my feet. A small plastic tube dangling inside the plastic jug fed the engine fuel. Such was often the norm of public transportation in this part of West Africa.

During our final month, I suffered from a terrible rash from head to toe, possibly due to the heat or an allergy to mangos. But despite taking antihistamines, the rash persisted and consumed my energy. The sedative effects of the medications I took didn't help. Like the Apostle Paul in the Bible suffered from what he called a *"thorn in the flesh,"* [1] this rash dampened my spirits. I was continually drained, lacking the motivation to do anything. Discouragement continued to set in. Then, one day, the teenage boy, Brahiim, whom I had been feeding daily and nursing back to health, made a turn for the worse and died. It hit me like a ton of bricks. Despite my best efforts, he passed anyway. Would any good come of it? I didn't know.

That same morning, I woke up with a headache. By that afternoon, I realized something was not right. My headache had not gone away despite trying to sleep unsuccessfully. I felt a knot forming in my stomach, so I took an antacid. At lunchtime, my head was splitting as if a vice was squeezing it, gradually building up more and more pressure. I sat at the table, but the sight of food made me bend over with nausea. I soon became dizzy and could barely make it to the bedroom without falling.

Jackie got me a pain reliever, and I took my weekly dose of Chloroquine, a common medication taken at that time to help prevent malaria. Lying in bed, the pressure in my head worsened, and my body temperature rose until I finally broke out in a sweat. I closed my eyes and drifted into a half-sleep. In a semi-conscious state, I wondered if this was the end. I tried to focus on God's presence, but I had difficulty thinking clearly and eventually drifted off.

Hours later, I awoke feeling better but still could not stand up. My temperature continued to rise again – 100.2, 100.4, 100.8 – and the headache returned stronger. Intense stomach cramps followed. Believing I was suffering from malaria, I asked Jackie to give me some injectable malaria medication and more fever medication. After that, I was able to sleep on and off again, but each time I awoke, the room spun around, and my eyes couldn't focus on anything. Whatever it was, I remained in bed for days. It took several weeks to regain my strength. Thankfully, the rash disappeared.

Soon, by late May, the unrelenting and stifling 110-degree Fahrenheit heat gave way to cooler temperatures. The seasonal Harmattan winds carrying the dust of the Sahara Desert into the atmosphere shrouded the sky, and clouds began to form in preparation for the rainy season. A thin layer of red dust covered every plant, tree, and bush. The dry, cracked terrain seemed to cry out to quench its thirst. The tips of the tall palms swayed in the wind as the low rumble of thunder echoed in the distance. Low, floating clouds came rolling in from the ocean as the wind moved more fiercely.

Then, in a moment of eerie silence, the slight patter of raindrops began. At first, they barely made small craters in the dust. Gradually, the rain poured more intensely and boldly until a rushing noise descended upon the land, and all the sky seemed like a solid sheet of water beating down on the steel roof, sounding like a freight train. The first rain of the season was truly a spectacular sight. A large mob of village children came running around the house, rejoicing and shouting at the arrival of the rain, some dancing around naked.

As I slowly recovered from my first bout with malaria, my courage was restored. My discouragement gave way to insight, and I could see more clearly how God might be able to use my skills in a place like this. I strongly sensed that God was opening a door for me to step forward in faith and return to West Africa as a part of the PBT team. It wasn't exactly what I had expected, yet the door of opportunity was open, so I chose to walk through it.

Yolanda and one of our other Dallas roommates, Barb, decided to come to West Africa after finishing more training. The plan was for me to return in a year after raising financial support and gaining more proficiency in French. Then, I would be assigned to assist churches in three language groups to develop literacy materials and programs. After that, the plan was for me to join Brent, Ellen, Yolanda, and Barb to further develop the literacy program we had started and assist with the translation project.

After returning to the US, I hired a French tutor and diligently studied French for nine months while I worked in a pediatric rehab center as a nurse to save up some money. Then I spent three months in France to improve my French fluency. Finally, after a successful time in France, I returned to West Africa as a full-time literacy consultant and nurse in May of 1991. I was 25, semi-fluent in French, fearless and confident.

Chapter Five

SEEDS OF FEAR

When I first returned to West Africa, Brent and Ellen were nursing a sick African child back to health in their home. Clearly, they were exhausted, so I gladly volunteered to help. However, after several weeks, I, too, became exhausted. My body succumbed once more to an illness of some sort, with abdominal pain, nausea, fever, and headache. Nevertheless, I recovered and prepared to take on my new assignment: consulting my first of three literacy projects in the country's interior.

The location for my first assignment was a two-day journey from the coast, in a more forested region, at a school for pastoral students. It was, thankfully, much cooler and more pleasant than the hot, muggy climate of the coast. The trip was long and exhausting because of the severely deteriorated roads, yet the scenery most of the way was breathtaking and refreshing.

As my colleague and chauffeur drove his fossil of a Land Rover over the endless potholes, I bounced out of my seat, hitting my head repeatedly on the vehicle's ceiling. I found it strangely exhilarating to embark on this new adventure, "roughing it" in the more rural parts of the country, referred to as the "African bush." My excitement grew as I anticipated what lay ahead. We finally arrived at the school compound where I was to live and work, and I was taken to my new living quarters. My new home was comfortably isolated from other houses and furnished with basic amenities. Grateful to have finally arrived, I slept well.

I settled into my new living situation and quickly made friends with my new African neighbors and the other expatriates working at the school. Everyone was enthusiastic the first time I was introduced at the local, thriving church. The church ladies welcomed me with dancing and singing. I was given a seat of honor customary for guests and workers from other countries. The women played on calabash tambourines, and young boys used virtually every part of their hands and arms to play their hand-crafted djembe drums. The intricate rhythms of the music mesmerized me.

Two young pastoral students, Jean Faya and Daniel, were chosen to be my assistants. Over the first nine months, we pored over word lists, created a dictionary, analyzed the sound structures, and formulated reading lessons until we had completed the rough draft of a primer series. With a few lessons drafted, I began teaching a reading class with 17 women whose husbands were studying to be pastors. I also trained some of those ladies as literacy teachers.

I met periodically with a committee of church leaders from various language dialects. They eventually agreed upon common terms, and together, we designed a teacher training program. I found it easy to get to know people and began learning some of the local language and customs. I could see God opening many doors, and I was thriving.

Without a car, I got around by bush taxis, bus, or hitching a ride with someone who had a vehicle. I grew accustomed to riding on the dusty roads in open-air taxis (meaning they had no windows), often packed with three times more people than the car was designed to carry. Of course, there were no seatbelts. I occasionally heard stories of the frequent fatal accidents on the winding, mountainous roads. Despite this, I fearlessly trusted that God would protect me from harm. These bush taxi adventures were full of opportunities to learn language, make friends, and share my faith.

During my time in the forest region, I began hearing stories of the war that had been going on for some time in a neighboring country. Refugees were fleeing, and over time I met quite a few of them who told me horror stories of what they witnessed and lived through. One man recounted how rebels had come to his village and started shooting at everyone. The villagers fled into the bush, not knowing where they would end up. This young man got lost and separated from his family, wandering for weeks, living off whatever he could find to eat in the wild and drinking dirty river water. By the time he arrived in our town, he was starving and sick with intestinal parasites. The young man almost died, but he survived thanks to some Christians in the town who nursed him back to health.

Hearing one story after another seared disturbing images in my mind. It seemed unfathomable that such horrors were happening not geographically far from where I lived and worked. Yet the danger seemed far removed from me – somehow unable to touch me. That is what I imagined, at least. My mind not want to consider anything else.

I hired one of the young pastoral students to translate some materials into the local language. He was quite a bold and powerful orator and had begun to preach openly in the marketplace in the nearby town. However, his preaching created quite a stir. Several people had come to him, saying they wanted to follow Jesus. Rumors circulated that many of the non-believers who opposed his message had put a curse on him. The young man said that now demons were following him around, wanting to drown him every time he walked by the river, and he could only stop them by singing Christian hymns out loud. He was unable to sleep for fear of harm from them. Many of the other pastoral students also became fearful.

It never occurred to me that followers of Jesus would be afraid that a curse or evil spirits could harm them, yet here they were, living in a culture where evil spirits were a part of their daily lives. This was a very real fear to them. I didn't fully understand how demons can oppose and oppress believers in Christ in tangible ways. I encouraged the student that God's power was stronger and that he had nothing to fear. I reminded him of the Apostle John's words that greater was he that was in them as followers of Christ than the evil one that is in the world.[1] In my mind, God would protect them, and even me, from all harm, just as he had Daniel, Paul, Peter, and others whose stories of faith were recorded in the Bible, if we trusted him.

But I would soon understand better that freedom from danger was not guaranteed for a follower of Christ. Sure, there was the accident in which the missionary was killed, but Brent and Ellen's son lived. I unconsciously bargained with God to keep me safe. I did not want to think too hard about the potential danger around me. I prayed for safety and trusted all would be well.

On one occasion, I needed to travel back to the coast to handle some paperwork for our organization. Since Brent and Ellen had returned stateside for a furlough, I also wanted to check on the child they had nursed back to health. It surprised me that a small airline company flew from this region to the coast, so I booked a flight on a small, 50-passenger plane. On the day of the flight, however, I realized that they had over-booked the flight. Without telephone communication between airports, the agents could not know how many empty seats were available. As a result, they habitually issued tickets to everyone who arrived, and some passengers would end up disappointed and unable to board the plane.

The airport was carved out of the jungle on the outskirts of town. As I waited, I stood in a growing throng of would-be passengers on the gravel runway. Everyone began pushing toward the plane and shouting at the flight attendant. As the crowd continued pushing past me, I wondered if I would be able to leave at all. Fortunately, the flight attendant saw me refusing to join in the chaos but attempting to avoid getting trampled.

He signaled to me, "*Mademoiselle, vous voyagez?*" (Young lady, are you traveling?)

I nodded, "*Oui.*"

He pushed back the crowd and ushered me onto the plane. It embarrassed me to be chosen over the rest of the people. I imagined they would all start rushing toward me in protest. Thankfully, they did not.

Once aboard the already-overcrowded plane, however, I could feel the stifling heat and lack of airflow. I found my seat, only to discover that a child accompanied by a woman with a bag of rice and a large bundle of bananas already occupied it. For a moment, I again worried that this trip might not happen. But the flight attendant made two children sit together to make room for me. I was grateful, yet a bit nervous.

I sat there in disbelief at all the people, baggage, and even chickens crammed into that plane. Everyone, including me, was sweating profusely. Some people stood in the aisle without a seat. No one seemed to think any of this was unusual. Were we really going to take off like this? They closed the doors, the engines revved up, and we took off with the plane's tail dragging low under the excessive weight.

We stopped at another town where more passengers expected to get on the plane. The pilot got angry and ran down the aisle, yelling at people and pushing people to get off so that others would have room to board. Soon afterward, he started up the engine while people were still disembarking. At that point, I began praying for the pilot and our safety. Thankfully, we landed at our destination without incident.

Several weeks later, when it was time for my return flight to leave at 6:00 a.m., I hired a taxi to pick me up at the guesthouse and take me to the airport early. It was still dark. As we pulled up to the airport curb and I exited the taxi, a gang of teenage boys approached me, asking to help me with my luggage. When I refused, one of them got angry and started shoving me and pulling on my shirt. I got back in the taxi and asked the taxi driver to pull ahead away from the gang. But the angry young man reached into the window, grabbed my purse with all my money in it, and ran off. I yelled, "Thief!" and urged the other boys to run after him. Instead, they just sauntered off. I felt violated and in shock.

Desperately, I turned to the taxi driver, asking him if he could help me. But he clearly didn't want to get involved. He shrugged and said these things happen. For a moment, I wondered if he had been in on it. Furious and shaken, I wandered toward the airport terminal, wondering how to pay the airport tax required to board the plane. I felt alone and stranded. By God's grace, another expatriate worker, Eric, whom I knew, showed up for a flight a few minutes later and paid my fare.

When our plane arrived, there was a mad rush of passengers toward it. I got pressed against a gate by the mob and could hardly breathe. Moments later, I was nearly trampled. The flight was again overbooked, and people were yelling and screaming. I told myself I would never fly this airline again if I survived. But just like the last time, one of the flight attendants summoned me to the front of the line and got me a seat.

We sat in the hot airplane on the runway for about an hour this time. The plane sat in the tropical heat with no ventilation or air conditioning, and the temperatures inside rose to what felt like 120 degrees Fahrenheit. I felt like I was going to pass out. The flight attendant kept squeezing kids in between people and on the floor. Eventually, the plane took off and then landed safely at our destination.

When I arrived back home, I talked to one of the senior missionaries about what had happened when the gang robbed me and pushed me around at the airport. He was unsurprised and even seemed indifferent, which made me feel even more alone and confused. I sensed that if I was to survive here as a single woman, I was expected to toughen up and suck it up. And that's what I did. I convinced myself that it was more spiritual to stuff it and keep it to myself. I feared that sharing my emotions with others would make me appear weak and dependent, and I did not want to be labeled as a complainer or regarded as a burden. But I didn't deal with the trauma and the fear growing inside me. I even felt shame that I was bothered by what happened – that others would think less of me. So, I kept up the appearance that I was okay. Deep inside, I felt inferior and misunderstood.

Now, only five months into my new assignment, the novelty was gone, and the warm welcomes ended. The honeymoon was over, as they say. Letters from friends back home were coming less often. I realized that people back home had moved on with their lives, and I was very alone in an unfamiliar place. The trauma I experienced gave me a taste of a reality I was unprepared for. Feelings of loneliness sank in, even when others were around. I had given up so much and was left feeling empty.

I tried to cling to God in those moments and to lean on his sufficiency. I learned to find joy in simplicity and in the friendships I had formed with some of my African neighbors and other expatriate workers. I began planting flowers, quilting, and pursuing other hobbies, learning to take a rest time for myself. I got a cat and was also taking care of another family's monkey while they were on furlough. All these distractions did help for a time.

Now a pet owner, I realized that I would need to find a way to get these pets vaccinated for rabies. Rabies was a real threat in that part of the world, and the story of a Peace Corps worker dying of rabies from her puppy reached my ears. I had heard that there was a vet in the capital where I could purchase refrigerated rabies vaccines. So, on one of my trips there, I ventured into the city by taxi. I was walking down the city's back roads to find this elusive vet clinic when I saw a young man walking in my direction. I suddenly realized I was all alone on this long, secluded street except for the man walking toward me. Fear welled up inside me, but I tried not to show it. I greeted the young man in the local language as he passed by. When the man stopped in front of me, my anxiety cranked up a notch. He asked me for my money. I told him that I didn't have much with me and...

Before I could finish my sentence, he reached down and ripped the watch from my wrist, jolted away from me, then began casually strolling down the road. My heart racing and my head spinning, I tried to keep my cool as I contemplated what I should do next. I was both frightened and angry. Just then, a pick-up truck full of men came around the corner and down the street toward me. I flagged them down and told them what had happened, pointing out the young man as he walked out of sight down the next street.

The men jumped into action quickly. Several stayed with me to keep me "safe," while the others went after the young thief. About five minutes later, they returned with my watch, the wristband now broken. They told me they had "taken care of" the young man. They apologized for his rude behavior toward me, a foreigner, as they put it, and gave me some money to buy a new wristband. Though grateful to have my watch back, I now felt terrible. My trauma-associated shame once again came into play as I began to worry about what had become of the young man. I hoped they didn't punish him too harshly, or worse, beat him to death. My cheap little watch was certainly not worth a young man's life. My emotions vacillated between satisfaction and guilt.

On another occasion in the capital, I set out to visit the large market searching for supplies I couldn't find elsewhere. By this time, I was accustomed to the routine of catching taxis. I knew all the usual taxi routes and was well-versed in using special hand signals locals used to wave down a taxi going in my direction. So, I flagged down a cab and headed toward the market. I noticed that many shops were closed on the way, but I paid no mind.

Not long after getting in the taxi, the driver stopped. All the vehicles were gridlocked in front of us. No one could move forward or backward. Suddenly, we could hear shouting up ahead and saw mobs of people running in our direction. I asked the taxi driver what was happening. Leaning out the window to listen, he could hear the crowds chanting, urging one another to attack the foreign merchants. One of them had apparently insulted an African earlier. He looked at me with a worried look on his face. He told me I could easily be mistaken for one of these foreigners and that I wasn't safe.

I panicked and begged him to get me out of there. However, he insisted that we were stuck, and he couldn't move the taxi. The mob kept drawing closer, and I became frantic. I urged him to try and move the car, giving him specific instructions on how he might be able to maneuver the vehicle in a way to break free. Finally, he started inching the taxi back and forth repeatedly until he rotated into the opposite lane. We sped away from the mob scene just in the nick of time. Seconds later, the mob descended upon the very spot where we had been.

The taxi driver tried to calm me down, but I was visibly shaking. After he dropped me off at the guesthouse, I was still shaking. When I informed one of the Americans residing at the guesthouse about what had happened, I got the same response as before: indifference. There was no debriefing. No processing. Only a sense that I should get over it. That was the risk I took, after all, living in this part of the world. Get used to it.

Again, my trauma was neither acknowledged by others nor dealt with. I felt shame for even going to the market. And I felt very alone. I tried to be brave and keep up appearances so I would not be seen as unspiritual.

Back home in the interior, I returned to my routine and threw myself into my work, trying to forget the trauma I had experienced in the capital. Christmas time came, and many of the missionaries and African Christians nearby prepared a delicious meal from the foods we had available. I enjoyed the fellowship and joy of the season with my new adopted family and friends for the first time. Life returned to its normal, slow, and laid-back pace.

By the end of February 1992, I was wrapping up my time on the first literacy project and preparing to move about six hours south to begin consulting on my second language project. I had just returned from another exhausting trip to the capital, where I visited several government offices and handled some challenging administrative issues. In the capital, I discovered that I contracted lice, either from the overcrowded public transportation I took or from the pet monkey I was caring for. In addition, my cat had died suddenly, which left me feeling more down than usual.

I was leaving home and friends behind once more. The layers of stress, illness, transition, and loss began to get to me and triggered depressed thoughts. Looking back, I realize not being able to process both recent and past traumas and grief contributed to my emotions. The first project had been extremely productive and successful, but I was weary and emotionally spent.

My next project was further south in an even more remote and forested region. The journey there took me through some of the last remaining untouched rainforests in West Africa. The road cut through layers upon layers of the tallest canopy trees I had ever seen. The dense, dark forest stretched on for miles in every direction over the mountainous terrain. I felt privileged and in awe to witness this piece of nature. Sadly, this part of the forest would be destroyed in the coming years as trees would be cleared for new refugee settlements and expanding development.

I stayed with a couple of other single missionary ladies for a few months in a newly built house in a large town. Living in this new environment was quite an adjustment. I slowly learned my way around the new market and adjusted to many changes. Meat was scarce and mostly sold under the table through private connections. By the time the remains reached the market, I had to stand in a long line behind dozens of pushing and yelling people, waiting to see if there would be any left to buy. Often there was none. The lack of quality food became a major stressor for me.

With all the walking I now had to do, my cheap plastic shoes, which I had purchased months before, had already worn out. So, one day I walked the 30 minutes to the market in town, intending to find something more durable. I was happy to find a leather shoe craftsman along the roadside who agreed to make me more durable leather sandals just my size for a reasonable price. We set a pick-up time for the next day around 11 a.m.

The following day around 10:30, I headed out the door toward the market. No sooner had I walked out of the gate than I heard the other two ladies I lived with start yelling out for help. I rushed back into the compound and discovered that the city water had just come on for the first time. Water was leaking everywhere, quickly flooding the house. As this house was new, the pipe fittings had never been tightened. It was customary to wait until the water came on to call the plumber, who would then come and tighten the pipes as needed.

I quickly abandoned all hopes of getting my shoes that day and joined the other ladies. Together the three of us ran about the house with buckets trying to contain the water until the plumber arrived. We managed to turn off most of the leaks inside the house, while the outside leak slowly turned the yard into a swamp. After three days, the plumber still had not shown up.

The next day when I finally went to pick up my sandals, the shoe vendor's little roadside kiosk had disappeared. I asked a nearby vendor if he knew where it was. He told me that a market truck had crashed into the kiosk the previous day, destroying it and killing two men standing in front of it. Thankfully the shoe vendor had survived and moved his business elsewhere. I eventually found him and got my shoes, but that was the least of my concerns. He informed me that the accident had happened around 11:00 a.m., precisely when I would have been standing there buying my shoes had the water not come on in the house. I shuddered at the thought of how close I had come to being killed. I decided not to complain about inconveniences and was grateful that God had protected me.

After the stress of the move, I was happy to take a break and visit some colleagues in a neighboring country. This required me to travel by bush taxi across the border. There were rumors of hassles at the border because of the war going on in that region. I wasn't sure if I should travel or not. However, I went in faith, trusting I could get a visa and cross over safely, arranging for colleagues to meet me on the other side. Thankfully, everything went smoothly.

However, I was curious when I saw an entourage of fancy vehicles pass through. When I asked who this was, the taxi driver informed me that it was one of the leaders of the factions in the war in that region. Having heard of the atrocities this man was responsible for, I was a little unsettled to come so close to him and his cohorts.

Once united with my colleagues across the border, we visited some beautiful waterfalls in that region. It did me some good to share with them openly about my experiences, particularly those I realized were traumatic. Unfortunately, while there, I became ill again with malaria and was hospitalized for several days. Still, my time with them was refreshing. After my health improved, I attended a conference on West Africa's southern coast. Our hotel had modern amenities and air conditioning. This was a big treat.

Refreshed by my little vacation, I had to travel back to the interior and across the country to another conference 2000 km (about 1200 miles) away. Word got around that I was heading that way, so friends with the United Nations High Commission for Refugees (UNHCR) asked me to drive one of their new vehicles across the two countries to deliver it to their colleagues.

This task seemed quite daunting, considering the territory and terrain I would have to navigate alone, especially near a war zone. I felt no small amount of anxiety but prayed about it and placed the trip in God's hands. Thankfully, I found several other Americans needing transportation, and they accompanied me for portions of the trip. Then, safely across the border, I traveled to the coast to attend the conference and spiritual retreat.

Chapter Six

OUR HELP IN AGES PAST

During the conference in the capital, I joined a group of friends and colleagues on a trek into the city to have ice cream at a favorite restaurant. Afterward, we piled into the four vehicles it took to carry us home. I sat next to a woman named Janice in the back seat of one of the vehicles. Janice and her husband had just arrived in the country only two weeks earlier. She held her two-month-old son in her lap while her husband sitting beside her held their three-year-old son.

Traveling back to the guesthouse, we were all laughing, engrossed in pleasant conversation. Then, suddenly, broken glass exploded outside the car. We could see dozens of small fires burning and a mob of young men throwing small bottles of ignited fuel, affectionately known as "Molotov cocktails."

At that, the driver yelled, "Get down!" Before I could duck, a large rock flew through the window beside me and hit my chest. I ducked my head down to my knees as thousands of pieces of window glass shattered around me and embedded themselves into my hair. More rocks came from other directions, causing a large shard of glass to stab Janice's husband in the shoulder. We heard people yelling, "White people!" in the local language and knew it was bad.

As I kept my head down, trembling, I could tell by the shaking and jerking movements of the vehicle that the driver was having difficulty navigating through the mob closing in on all sides. I couldn't see anything. In my heart, I feared the worst. I wondered if this was it, if we were all going to die. My previous experience with an enraged mob taught me they couldn't be controlled.

Then Janice began singing, "*O God, our help in ages past, our hope for years to come; our shelter from the stormy blast, and our eternal home.*" The rest of us joined in. It took every ounce of courage I could muster to even control my breathing, let alone sing in my panicked state. But it seemed like a good thing to do.

Miraculously, our vehicle cleared the crowd within minutes, and we were on our way back to the guesthouse. Safely back, we realized that our caravan was short one vehicle. In those days, we did not have cell phones or radios for communication. We all sat around worried, wondering if the others were okay. Eventually, we received a note from a messenger that they were safe. They had diverted down a different road to find safety at another colleague's home.

We laid low over the next few days, hearing about other incidents where foreigners were attacked and harmed. The US Embassy advised us not to leave home until they informed us it was safe to travel in the city again. At one point, they told us we might need to evacuate. However, within a few days, the city's atmosphere returned to normal as if nothing had ever happened. We were shaken but thankful everyone was safe and could return to our different work locations.

Looking back, I wondered how Janice had the presence of mind to think of singing a hymn during all that chaos. Years later, I asked her about it. She told me that she grew up in Vietnam where her parents served. She was in a similar situation there. The event stuck with her for years. This hymn had taken on special meaning because of what she had gone through. It gave her the courage to cope as she was reminded of God's presence and help in times of danger. "*O God, our help in ages past, our hope for years to come; our shelter from the stormy blast, and our eternal home.*" She had practiced this response to the point where it had become instinctive. I realized I had no plan for reacting to a crisis except panic. I had a lot to learn.

As I reflected on this hymn, its lyrics served as a reminder that God is with us in every situation, even the dangerous, chaotic ones. He has been with us in the past, even when we can't see him. He is with us now, and he will be with us in the years to come. When everything crumbles around us, we can hold on to the truth that he is sturdy and worthy of our trust. I had to flood my mind with these words of truth. I needed to focus on Jesus.

Deep inside, however, doubts began creeping in. Will he shelter us from the blast? I wrestled with this. Yes, he did protect us that night. Yes, he protected me as I crossed the border. Yes, he healed me from various illnesses when I felt near death. He kept me from being crushed by the mob at the airport and from being plowed over by an out-of-control truck in the marketplace that day when I was hoping to pick up my shoes. But what about other times when he allowed people, even missionaries, to be harmed?

The reality of this hit me hard, and I could no longer ignore it after this most recent event. I thought of so many people who had died serving God, even in this country. And throughout history, hundreds of thousands of believers have been martyred as they stood unwavering in their faith. What about them? If God didn't protect them, would he protect me? Could I trust him?

I was encouraged by the fact that we were saved from potential disaster this time. But subconsciously, my confidence began eroding. My fear grew under the surface. I had had too many close calls, and they were having their effect on me. These incidents seemed to be happening more frequently and with greater intensity.

A few days after the incident, I drove along that same route to town. I noticed a few shops which were usually open were now closed. It triggered me: I remembered there was trouble the last time shops were closed. I froze. I pulled over and couldn't go any further. A tremendous sense of dread came over me. My heart started racing, and my chest felt tight. I was afraid to drive into town. No one had reported unrest. But something told me I should not go any further. Was it just my fear? Or was there real danger? I really didn't fully understand what was happening. Should I turn back, or should I go into town? Finally, I decided to turn back and return to the guesthouse. Maybe it was nothing. I just couldn't take a chance.

Later I learned that there was indeed unrest in town that day. This confirmed my suspicion and reinforced my instincts to respond cautiously and trust my fears. Whenever I got an uneasy feeling, I began trusting that feeling and avoided potentially stressful or dangerous situations. Fear began dictating my decisions and my actions.

Over the next couple of years, a strange feeling would come over me whenever I drove back through that intersection where we had been attacked. Most of the time, I paid no attention to it. But it was still there. The hairs on the back of my neck would stand up. Later in the day, I would get a headache. Sometimes I would feel short of breath. I tried to shake the feeling, and many times I was just fine.

But other times, I wasn't. Though I didn't realize it then, my brain was developing neural responses to trauma that interfered with my normal functioning. Previously known as "shellshock," the label "Post Traumatic Stress Disorder" became an official diagnosis in 1980.[1] Even so, it was not widely used in the early 90s as it is today. Little did I know that the stressful events of my first few years in Africa, combined with childhood experiences, faulty coping mechanisms, and perhaps some flawed theology, paved the way for PTSD, anxiety, and fear to become deeply rooted within my psyche.

A month after the attack, I was back in the forest region. I had primers from the first literacy project printed and in hand. The next step was to develop teacher training tools to use them. I spent several weeks living with an African family in a village where Jean Faya and his wife had been assigned to lead a church. Jean Faya and I worked tirelessly there to finish the teacher training books. Following this, we held our first teacher-training workshop, to which all the local churches in that language group sent delegates. I sensed great enthusiasm for literacy from the attendees, and several leaders actively took ownership of their local programs. Things were progressing nicely, and I was confident I was leaving the project in good hands.

At the end of the summer, my family offered to fly me home to the US for a month to attend a family reunion. During the whole road trip back to the coast for my flight, I was nauseous and knew something was wrong. Once in the capital, I went to see a doctor. She diagnosed me with an intestinal parasite that affected my appetite. I had most likely picked it up while living in the village the month before. After she gave me a treatment, my appetite slowly improved.

When I stepped off the plane in St. Louis, I was glad to see family and friends there to greet me. However, instead of the expected enthusiasm, they all looked concerned, alarmed at how thin I had become. Since I didn't have a scale in Africa, I had not realized how much weight I had lost from my recent illness. At 5 foot 7 ½ inches tall, I was now close to 110 pounds, and it showed in my appearance.

Fortunately, a month in the US was all it took to return to my normal weight. While in the US, I participated in a strategy meeting with our growing PBT West Africa team. There were now six families and four singles, including Barb, Yolanda, and me. It was exciting to be a part of this growing team.

When I returned to West Africa, I experienced election-related civil unrest for the first time. Unfortunately, it would not be the last. For the next 17 years, civil unrest would become a regular occurrence. The expatriate and missionary community made contingency plans, prayed a lot, and tried to stay out of harm's way while remaining productive. This became a way of life in our region.

Over the next few months, I worked alongside other missionaries interested in starting literacy projects in the forest region, helping them rough draft primers for yet another language group. I also wrapped up my other projects enough to head back to the coast. There, I would work again with Brent and Ellen, who would soon return, as would Yolanda and Barb. My excitement grew in anticipation.

I spent a week preparing Brent and Ellen's village house for all of us to move in. I quickly discovered that in West Africa, when you move out, other creatures move in. The amount of damage little critters could do in one year was astonishing. The mice chewed through cement and Tupperware, destroying what little food had been stored. Mud daubers had built nests in virtually every corner and on some furniture. Termites had set up residence in the bookshelves, building their mud nests behind all the books and feasting on the pages.

Then, one day while working in the house, I was startled by crunching and scraping sounds in a bedroom I hadn't yet cleaned. I slowly opened the door and saw two beady eyes peering at me from behind the door. I mustered up the courage to go inside and see for myself. It turned out to be a large crab that had come up from the estuary and had sandwiched itself between the door and some boxes. I decided to make the most of it and cook him for dinner.

Soon after my teammates arrived, we found a village house for me to rent, and my colleagues helped me get things set up. Two older men who lived in a hut across from my house were designated as my "protectors." The house was in bad shape but had lots of potential. Over the next few months, I hired local workers to do repairs, install bathroom plumbing, and paint the whole house. We remedied the nightly visits from the local rats by putting up screens on all the windows.

I began enjoying village living and made good progress learning the local language. Barb and Yolanda set up their own home in a neighboring village, and we all settled into our new routines. Together, we celebrated holidays and birthdays per our American tradition, doing our best to make familiar recipes with available ingredients. Our laughter, fellowship, and familiar traditions were great diversions. They helped us cope with the never-ending challenges and culture stress of living in this part of West Africa.

Before long, I set up a little front-porch medical clinic and began seeing patients. I primarily treated burn patients, continuing the work that Jackie had done several years prior. Soon, a steady stream of patients came daily, sometimes from as far as two hours away. People would come at random times most days, often interrupting my work on literacy materials. I finally tried to designate "clinic hours," which seemed to work better.

One day a young mother brought me her premature baby boy. The mother had stopped feeding the infant, who was weak and frail. I had difficulty not becoming emotional as I watched the baby look around helplessly with questioning eyes and a barely audible cry. The child was clearly near death, and I lacked the resources to save him. Once, another woman named Mamata brought her two-year-old child who was skin and bones and covered in boils. The mother herself was emaciated. This wasn't characteristic of women in this culture, who were usually well-fed from the abundant fresh foods. I knew something more was wrong.

After the child died, the grandmother came to me, saying Mamata was asking for me. She had grown so weak she could not get out of bed and was also covered with boils. She said her husband had left her long ago. Everyone, even family, had abandoned her and were waiting for her to die, not even feeding her. The idea that your fate is sealed, regardless of how you try to change it, was prevalent in this culture.

Such "fatalism" often influenced people's decisions on whether to seek medical treatment. In addition, illness was sometimes viewed as a curse or the judgment of God.

Horrified, I knew Mamata's only chance of living was in my care. I took her to a doctor in the city who diagnosed her with multiple tumors and tuberculosis. He also suggested that she had AIDS, but he could not confirm this because no testing was available. He said the family likely suspected it as well, but admitting an AIDS diagnosis was shameful to them. I took her home, and I prayed over her. She was so sad and knew her time was short. I cried most of the day, asking God to show me what to do. I felt helpless, outraged at the family's response, and frustrated that she had run out of options.

Then I told her about my hope in Jesus. She asked me to tell her more about Jesus so she could also believe. And so I did. As I shared with her my hope in Jesus, she professed her faith in him right there. I had to travel away for several days on a trip, and when I returned, I found that she had passed away.

Stories like this were all-too-common scenarios that I experienced regularly. Yet, as many of my colleagues would attest, with each situation, there came amazing opportunities to show Christ's love to people. We had a strong sense of being used by God but also a tremendous sense of grief over the suffering in this part of the world. One day I decided to start asking women in our village of about 3,000 people how many children they had borne and how many were living. Over time, I discovered that the average mother had lost 50% of children born to her. This was the sad reality for these families. Death became a regular occurrence, especially the death of children. People often brought sick children or family members to my clinic when it was far too late to save them.

We had no reliable laboratory nearby to diagnose anything. Treating patients was often a guessing game for which my nursing training did not prepare me. I sometimes referred patients to another clinic or hospital, but they usually wouldn't go because they couldn't afford treatment there. Or they came to me as a last resort after the clinics or hospital had exhausted treatment options. Making life-and-death decisions on my own weighed heavily on me. With each situation, I prayed that God would simply show Christ through me, if not heal my patients.

Additionally, recurring illness continued to be a routine part of my own life as well as my teammates. I lost consciousness with one bout of malaria and ended up again in the hospital. When I wasn't treating myself for malaria, a sinus infection, or an intestinal parasite, I was helping my colleagues treat theirs. We all sensed that Satan was using our sickness to discourage us. Thankfully, we met regularly as a team and prayed together. We talked openly about our struggles, debriefed, and supported each other through challenges. I was grateful to have them around. Still, there were some struggles that I had a hard time talking to anyone about.

In the spring of 1993, an international linguistic organization asked me to teach at a month-long seminar. Literacy leaders from ten West African countries gathered to train forty-some delegates, representing various language groups, in writing literacy materials. By this time, my French had improved tremendously, and I had used it to speak in small groups. But, at this event, I had to present a lecture in French to around 100 people, including ministers of education and other high-ranking officials. I would be speaking at a main session, which would be televised, no less.

I was a bit nervous, to say the least, and I wasn't sure my French was polished enough for the occasion. At that moment, the shy little girl who would refuse to get on stage so long ago was wondering how on earth she ended up here. I observed the other presenters before me and noted their behaviors, expressions, and mannerisms. I read over my notes, trying to fight the anxiety as I prepared to speak. Finally, it was my turn. I hoped to not make a fool of myself and tried to judge people's reactions from their expressions. They nodded as I spoke, and seemed to listen intently, so I assumed I was getting my point across. Either that, or they were being gracious and patient.

After my presentation, they assigned me a language group. I spent the rest of the month doing what I had now done four times: helping African nationals design literacy primers in their own language. The seminar was exhausting. Halfway through, a whole host of people got sick, including me. We had been consuming unfamiliar food, beverages, and apparently contaminated water the entire time. Several people were taken to the hospital or local clinics and diagnosed with dysentery.

In the fall of 1993, Yolanda and I were asked to lead several teacher training and writer workshops in the forest region. Without a decent vehicle to drive ourselves, we took a bus – a grueling and hot 18-hour trip straight through. The roads were winding and bumpy, even worse than the first time I had traveled them two years earlier. Halfway through the trip, I "lost my cookies" out the window. The African man sitting behind me gave me a look of disgust as I tried to regain my composure. We finally arrived at our destination at 1:30 a.m. Because it was so late, we spent the night on the bus at the taxi station. The bus driver was afraid to let anyone off for fear of bandits. Yolanda and I got little sleep that night.

Still exhausted from the trip and suffering from a queasy stomach, I found it difficult to teach during the conference. Several days into it, I began running a fever. A blood test showed I had malaria once again. What's more, I experienced a temporary loss of hearing while taking a quinine treatment for the malaria.

At the same time, six boils broke out in some not-so-pleasant places on my body. I wouldn't wish that on my worst enemy. I mused that God wanted me to empathize with my patients and their suffering. My mind went to the story of Job in the Bible. Six weeks of antibiotics later, I was finally rid of the boils, but my digestive tract was messed up for a long time afterward.

While we were leading the workshops, unrest between ethnic groups broke out once again on the coast. We were advised to avoid traveling back by road. We were eventually able to take a flight back.

Once I had returned to my village, the aftermath of the ethnic riots became apparent. A man wounded in the leg with a machete came to my clinic. The huge gash in his leg had festered for three days, so I treated him aggressively with antibiotics. Despite this, his lower leg began turning black, so I took him to the city to see a surgeon. The surgeon told me he would have to debride the wound and asked if I would like to assist. I agreed.

However, I was dismayed when the surgeon started cutting away at the man's leg. The surgeon had given the man no anesthesia, and he was still very much awake. The man tried bravely to hold back cries of agony, clenching his teeth and holding his breath. I could tell it was excruciating. Little by little, I watched in horror as the surgeon cut more and more of the flesh from the man's leg until all that was left was mostly bone in some places. I wondered how this man would ever be able to walk again, let alone survive the risk of infection.

At that point, I could no longer hold back the tears and wept openly. The suffering I witnessed that day was beyond imagination. The man survived, but he remained crippled and became a regular patient of mine for months to come.

In the following months, I continued developing literacy materials. Several of us set up literacy classes for our neighbors. Unfortunately, illness continued to wreak havoc on all of us. A typhoid epidemic landed two of my teammates in the hospital. We all had to make an extra effort to sanitize everything, drink only filtered water, and soak our fruits and vegetables in water mixed with iodine tablets or a small amount of bleach.

Chapter Seven

SHATTERED PEACE

In December 1993, I flew back to the US for the holidays to attend my brother's wedding. The visit was refreshing, but I realized how much I missed my village life – the village and West Africa had become home. I also missed my teammates. After all, we had been through so much together. Upon my return to Africa, we had a great reunion.

Despite the challenges I had faced living in Africa up to that time, I began to feel settled. I made my house a home and came to feel somewhat safe and at peace in my setting. I planted a garden, landscaped my yard, added some homey touches to my house, and got several more pets, including another cat, a parrot, and two wild genet kittens my teammates had given me. My daily life became more routine, and I enjoyed the literacy and medical ministry. At times, I could imagine myself living there for a long time.

One night, however, my sense of peace was once again shattered. A rhythmic scratching noise suddenly awakened me. Thinking it was the rats again, I got out of bed to investigate. As I entered the living room, I could hear the noise coming from outside the window. Having closed the indoor shutters for the night, I suspected the cat was trying to get in, so I opened them, only to discover two men standing on my windowsill, one wearing a red shirt. They were attempting to steal the solar panel I had wired onto my roof but were unsuccessful up to that point. I let out a blood-curdling scream, which echoed into the forest behind my house. The men quickly jumped down and ran off.

I called out to my landlady, who lived in a small room off my back porch. I could hear her yelling that she couldn't get out. The thieves had barred her door so she could not thwart their plans; she was trapped inside. Moments later, my "protectors" came to our rescue and let my landlady out of her room. Everyone was supportive and tried to comfort me and calm me down, but I could not calm myself.

One of the "protectors" agreed to stay outside that night and guard my house, but I still could not sleep. In fact, I didn't sleep for 10 days. I could sleep only after some visiting colleagues, Jay and Sue, came and stayed with me for a week. Having them around helped to make me feel safe, at least for the time being. But my fears and anxiety kept me hypervigilant and unable to truly relax. I found myself eyeing young men in the village suspiciously, especially those wearing red shirts, wondering if they were the thieves. To my knowledge, no one ever found out who they were. This left me with an uneasy feeling, fearful that they might return.

It was customary for members of our organization to return to their home country every three to four years for time away from the stresses of the field and to reconnect with family, friends, and financial supporters. Three years had passed, and my furlough time had arrived. I prepared for a nine-month return to the US.

Looking back over my first term in Africa, I realized it had been hard. I don't know where I found the courage to do some of the gutsy things I did. I went through many of those things alone, forcing me to lean more on God. I had accomplished a lot. I had been through trauma. I looked forward to the time of rest and recuperation that could take place on furlough.

However, my future seemed unclear. I was losing my vision and wondered where I should go from here. Although I had grown fond of my home and many things about my life and work, I wasn't sure how willing I was to return to Africa and endure more challenges alone. Knowing that others might not always be there to walk through things with me, my loneliness in the journey sank in hard.

Yes, God had provided colleagues and friends, both expatriates and Africans, to walk alongside me at different points in the journey. But once again, the longing for a soul mate to share life with dominated my thoughts. At 29 years old, I was not getting any younger. God had provided a whole village community of children to love on, yet I felt empty and longed to have my own children. I had prayed for a godly husband for years, but every possibility fizzled. Like the persistent widow Jesus talked about in the Gospel of Luke, chapter 18, I continued to commit the aches of my heart every night to God in prayer. More passionately than ever, I begged him not to send me back to West Africa alone.

Before returning home, I spent a month in Paris doing research for a master's thesis. While there, I telephoned my mother. With the poor communication infrastructure where I lived in West Africa, I rarely had that opportunity. My mom told me about an intern, Jim, serving at our church that summer. He had told her he was interested in overseas mission work. I was cautiously curious.

I arrived in St. Louis a month later, and my mother pointed Jim out to me the very next day at church. The pastor announced my return from Africa and made me stand up, and everyone applauded. Little did I know that Jim took advantage of the moment and finally got a good look at me. Apparently, some of our mutual friends had also been telling him about me.

I met Jim for the first time a few weeks later, and we struck up a conversation. He had served in the US Navy for eight years in the submarine force, but his military career was cut short when he lost a leg in a motorcycle accident. After that, Jim started Bible College and dedicated his life to ministry. He had joined the church's praise band as a guitarist. He seemed like a nice guy, and we had a lot of things in common.

Before long, I had agreed to go to a guitar concert with him which was still two months away. We spoke briefly over the next few months, and I got my hopes up. However, one night when my mother invited him over for dinner, he randomly commented that he hated the heat and could never go to Africa. My hopes were dashed. I wrote him off, thinking anyone who could say something like that would not be a good option for me. After all, I really hoped to go back to Africa. Oh well, I thought. I could at least have some fun going to the concert with him.

I had some very serious, heartfelt talks with God around that time. I was probably suffering from a bit of depression that lingered from the months of stress and illness I endured in West Africa, but I knew I was at a turning point in my life. I wept bitterly before the Lord, in anguish about my loneliness, even wishing God would take my life. Yet, despite these emotions, I held out hope that God could do anything, and I chose to remain obedient to him. I waited for him, even though the struggle was deep. I prayed for strength to get through it.

The night of the concert, I got all dressed up. Jim picked me up and took me to a nice dinner. Then we were off to the concert hall. The skill and artistry of the featured classical guitarist thrilled us both. We had delightful conversations all evening long, and I felt like I could talk to him about anything. As the night went on, I realized I didn't want it to end. After he dropped me off, I knew I didn't even want to entertain thoughts of any other man; all I could think about was Jim.

In the following months, Jim and I spent more and more time together, sometimes just meeting together to study. He was finishing his last year at Bible College, and I was taking seminary classes to complete my graduate degree. With each passing day, I knew that I could not imagine my life without him. However, a nagging question always hung in the back of my mind. What about that comment he made about never wanting to go to Africa?!

Finally, one night I confronted him. He admitted he made that remark half-heartedly but also said that he was sincerely open to going wherever God would lead him. Relieved, our conversation turned toward where our relationship was going. After a six-hour discussion over the phone, we mutually decided to begin an official courtship. I realized that it didn't matter where in the world I ended up serving; I only knew that I wanted to spend my life serving alongside Jim.

One month later, I was scheduled to speak at one of my partnering churches that supported my work in West Africa. As I was preparing the night before to share what God had done over those three years, I was uncertain what I would tell them about my future. Would I go back to Africa? If so, when? What would I do? As I gathered my thoughts together, there was a knock at the door. It was Jim holding his guitar. He started serenading me. I soon realized he was proposing to me. I said yes!

And just like that, my future had suddenly become a lot clearer. I shared the good news of our engagement with the partnering church the next day. I couldn't help but be grateful that God had worked everything out. He answered my prayers beyond what I could hope for and gave me a reason to continue. Why he chose to show his mercy toward me now, I didn't understand. Maybe it was to teach me to pray persistently and totally rely on him. But the answer had come, and I felt at peace.

Over the winter break of December 1994, Jim made plans to travel to West Africa to join my colleagues. He hoped to see if God could use him as part of the team there, particularly in the work of Bible Translation. During the month he was gone, I heard nothing from him, as he had no access to any telecommunication. I agonized over the silence and constantly worried about his safety. I knew he was going to some rough areas and that sickness was a real possibility. Waiting that month became a huge faith exercise for me, so I busied myself with wedding preparations.

The trip went amazingly well. Jim returned with a vision of what Bible Translation ministry could look like in West Africa. Since he had already excelled as a student of Biblical Greek, Jim's trip made him even more passionate about the work of PBT. We planned to get married in May, but Jim would have to complete the same training I had done before we headed overseas.

However, as we prepared for the wedding, we encountered some snags in our relationship. One thing led to another, and before long, we had trust issues. I became depressed once again. I wondered if Jim would really love me if he knew of my dark, depressive thoughts. We sought counseling and pored through marital counseling books. How could we know if this marriage was going to work out?

Then several things happened that changed our perspective. I realized the greatest challenge of my life was not going to Africa, learning another language, or any other past endeavor. The greatest challenge lay ahead of me: dying to myself and embracing a new life with this man who loved me so totally and completely. Jim was abandoned to God more than I was. He had flaws, as did I. But he was also surrendered to God's will. I had always prayed for a man of God's choosing. What if that man wasn't perfect? Was I willing to embrace all that he was, flaws and all? Was I being selfish? Could I surrender to the unknown again, this time to marriage, and learn to trust my husband-to-be with my future? I found myself resisting the transformation God wanted to do in me, to become selfless. Ultimately, I had to surrender once again if I was to move forward.

Then I was invited to attend a two-day symposium on depression and mental health for healthcare professionals in the St. Louis area. This topic interested me; it was an opportunity to learn more about myself than anything else. I hoped to gain insights that might help me overcome bouts with depression to which I was prone. From the conference, I better understood the role nutrition, vitamins, stress, and trauma had on mental health. I knew I would need to pay better attention to nutrition and rest. I started on a vitamin supplement, and my mood improved dramatically.

Also, as Jim and I read through counseling books, we read one thing that really jumped out at us. One author cited statistics that showed Christian couples had the same divorce rate as non-Christian couples. However, married couples who prayed together daily had less than a 1% divorce rate. When we read this, we realized we had talked about praying together but never really did. We made a commitment right then to start praying together and stay committed to it.

From then on, we determined never to let a day go by that we didn't come together, whether in person or over the phone, and pray aloud together. We slowly began to see how this helped everything fall into place. Our mutual trust grew stronger as our lives became more entwined with God at the center. We married in May and began our lives together.

Chapter Eight

A NEW BEGINNING

After the wedding, Jim and I were delighted as we embarked on our new journey together. We discussed having children and decided we wanted a large family. My anxiety and depression subsided for about a year. We spent three months in Oregon for Jim's studies, then moved to Dallas so he could continue. I worked for several home health agencies in the Dallas area to help pay for Jim's schooling. I enjoyed setting up our first apartment together and making it a home. Our marriage was off to a good start. We grew daily in our love and commitment to one another, and three months after our wedding, we were elated to learn that I was expecting our first child.

During my pregnancy, I continued to work every day, driving sometimes 200 miles a day to different homes around the Dallas/Fort Worth area to care for my patients. When I was 37 weeks pregnant, I noticed my ankles began to swell. I wasn't too alarmed, knowing this was somewhat normal in pregnancy. However, my coworkers at one of the agencies were concerned and offered to take my blood pressure. It was a bit high. My routine appointment with the doctor was only a few days away, so I waited.

On the day of my appointment, I was scheduled to see several patients for work, with my own doctor's appointment sandwiched in between. While driving to see my first patient, I began to feel strange and had waves of dizziness wash over me. I felt like I might pass out. Not sure if

I should pull over or what to do, I prayed. I got through my first patient appointment, then drove to the doctor's office. As I walked in, the staff immediately noticed my face and legs were swollen, and they could see I was not feeling well. A quick blood pressure check and a few other tests revealed I was in pre-eclampsia.

From that moment on, things moved very fast. The staff told me they would have to rush me over to the hospital immediately and induce labor. There wasn't even time to call my husband, they said. However, I insisted I would not have this baby without my husband present, so they agreed to let me make one quick phone call. Since he was in class and didn't have a cell phone, I left a message with the school operator to try and reach him.

Not knowing if Jim would show up for the birth of our first child, I was rushed off by the office staff to the hospital across the street to be admitted. Four hours later, I was in full-blown labor and had at least eight monitor cords, tubes, or IV lines attached to some part of my body. I was so grateful when Jim walked in the door with his smiling face. A few hours later, our daughter, Katie, was born. We were filled with joy and thankfulness.

With our new daughter in hand, I realized God had borne fruit of our decision to trust his will and surrender to one another in our marriage. Love was a choice and a chance worth taking. Our daily prayers kept us humble and honest before each other and before God. We learned more and more each day about trusting him. I shuddered to think what would have happened if I had held on to my pain and pride and decided not to marry Jim. I would never have experienced my husband's love, which I felt was God's way of slowly transforming me. Nor would I be holding this precious gift in my hands. I now had two reasons to live outside of myself. So much joy came from loving them and simply being with them.

A month after Katie's birth, we drove to northern Quebec, where we lived for the next 7 months so Jim could immerse himself in the French language and culture in preparation for ministry in French-speaking West Africa. I cared for Katie at home and helped drill Jim in his French lessons. The first four months with Katie were a bit rocky, as she developed colic and stayed awake all night. The lack of sleep began to wear on my emotions.

Thankfully, with a friend's help, we got her on a sleep schedule, and she became a very happy baby. With better sleep, my mood improved. By December, Jim had achieved the required level of French proficiency for ministry with PBT in West Africa, so we wrapped things up in Quebec and headed back to St. Louis for the holidays.

We were beyond excited at the prospect of returning to Africa together, so we wasted no time: we got our immunizations, began packing, and reserved our plane tickets for a February flight to West Africa. In addition to Barb and Yolanda, and Brent and Ellen, the PBT team in West Africa had grown to five families, including my brother and his wife. We hoped to start a translation and literacy project in a new language group. Jim would accompany another team on a survey trip of several language groups to help determine which one was best suited for our family.

However, on Christmas Eve, a home pregnancy test confirmed I was once again pregnant. Jim was ecstatic. Though excited about another child, I was not ready to be pregnant again. It had only been 7 months. I was concerned about how this would impact our return to Africa. Knowing that healthcare quality in West Africa was not so good, I feared having an experience similar to Katie's birth without adequate healthcare. Could I even go back to Africa pregnant? Then, at nine weeks of pregnancy, I had complications and was put on bed rest. At that point, we knew we would not be returning to Africa in February. Discouragement set in.

During the next 8 weeks on bed rest, I struggled again with anxiety and fear. I had frequent cramping, and I feared losing this baby. Each day seemed to drag on for an eternity without an end in sight. At times, I had difficulty remembering what it was like not to be pregnant. I tried to occupy myself by entertaining Katie from the couch as she explored her little world and moved through milestones.

The nagging fear of miscarrying cast a cloud over me most days. Church friends would come over bearing gifts of food and prayers. Most of the time, they were a great source of encouragement and helped me to pass the time. However, one well-meaning lady said she just knew from the first time I announced my pregnancy that this child was somehow different, as if to utter some bad omen. Never sure what she meant by that, but it did not help calm my fears.

After much prayer and a few phone calls, we decided Jim would travel to West Africa without me. He would go on the planned survey trip and return before the birth of our second child. I would stay with my mom, who would help care for Katie and me. So, in February, Jim flew to West Africa alone.

Thankfully, around 17 weeks of pregnancy, the doctor determined the greatest risk of danger in my pregnancy had passed, and I was allowed to get up and walk around. With Jim gone, I continued to take it easy. I enjoyed exploring local parks with my mom and Katie while my belly and the rest of me grew in size.

When Jim finally returned, we had an important decision to make about which language group we would choose as our project. We had two choices, each with pros and cons. One of the language groups was isolated in the forest region. This would be a brand-new project among a people group of about 18,000 where no one had ever worked before. It looked like a perfect fit for us.

The other was a much larger project involving the delicate politics of taking over a project that someone with a different organization had started. The people group numbered over 4 million. This project didn't appeal to us in any way, but everyone on our team encouraged us to take on this larger, higher-priority project. After considerable deliberation, prayer, and lengthy discussions with our colleagues, we agreed to work in the larger group.

Meanwhile, as I approached my 28th week of pregnancy, I began having strong and painful contractions close together. Jim rushed me to the hospital, where the staff worked all night to stop the contractions with medications. Thankfully, I had not dilated significantly, so I was sent home the next morning with medication and another order for bed rest. A few days later, they found that I had an infection and put me on antibiotics.

From then on, the remainder of the pregnancy was just difficult. Each day that went by was a countdown to the baby's arrival. Bedrest seemed to last an eternity. I wanted a healthy baby, of course, but I longed to not be pregnant anymore. Every day we wondered if I would go into early labor again and face having a premature baby with potential health complications. We also knew that this could potentially jeopardize our future service overseas. Once again, we had to exercise our faith by surrendering our lives and future into God's hands.

Around 34 weeks, my blood pressure went up again, so my doctor put more restrictions on my activity. Then, on August 10th, at 5 a.m., almost a month before I was due, my water broke. Contractions were mild, so Jim and I calmly packed our bags and headed to the hospital. Seven hours of labor later, I delivered our son, Joshua. He seemed so tiny. But we were thankful that he was healthy. We were grateful we had not tried to go through the pregnancy in Africa. We breathed a great sigh of relief and praised God. The hospital allowed us to take him home on the third day.

As he thrived and grew every day, we began making plans to return to West Africa.

This time we would be returning to West Africa with two small children. I had been so focused on bringing Joshua into the world that I had not thought much about the journey ahead. I had prayed for a husband, prayed for children, and prayed to return to Africa. God granted all that and more, but I discovered that I had new fears. As I held my precious little boy, tears formed in my eyes. Would we finally arrive back in Africa, only to have his little life taken away from us because of some tropical disease like malaria? I researched everything I could about some of the new anti-malarial drugs available, trying to find the yet-unpublished dosing information for infants and small children.

At one point, I even called an expert at the Centers for Disease Control. The woman I spoke to chided me for being so foolish as to take my children to that disease-ridden part of the planet. I resolved not to hang up without getting my answer. I reminded the expert that millions of African children were already suffering from those diseases. What about them? Why were my children so special? I needed the information, not only for my own children but also to help the hundreds of African children who would be brought to my door for treatment. Reluctantly, she agreed to help me and gave me the dosing information. Satisfied with my results, I crafted a plan, as best as I could, to protect my children from the diseases they would eventually encounter so we could remain healthy while we served overseas. I knew the dangers. Trusting God with these little ones he had given us would be the next biggest fear I would have to overcome.

As we prepared to leave, we rallied a team of prayer warriors all over the country to fight the spiritual battle that lay ahead and to cover us in prayer as we embarked on our journey. Finally, in October 1997, we were ready to leave. Katie was 18 months old, and Joshua was barely 2-1/2 months. Only God had made it possible for us to come this far. All that time, he kept our hope alive and strengthened us. We boarded the first of a series of planes on our journey back to West Africa, now as a family of four, filled with hope and expectation.

Chapter Nine

A ROCKY START

O ur first series of flights back to Africa was a big adjustment for Jim and me. We had months to pack and plan and were familiar with the trials of flying to Africa. We felt we had matters well in hand, but we were in for a big surprise.

We soon learned how challenging it was to travel internationally with two small children. Before we even got on the first flight, Katie, who had already missed naptime, started having a tantrum, screaming and crying. We tried to maneuver all our carry-ons with two babies. But things didn't work out like we planned. We asked for assistance in boarding. The flight attendant escorted me in with the two fussy kids first, leaving Jim to handle all the baggage alone. Then the attendant informed us that we had too many bags, despite what the airline had told us previously. She hassled us but finally let us take all our bags. Of course, all of this held up the impatient passengers behind us. We gave them all apologetic looks.

We had painstakingly tried to reserve the bulk-head seats with a baby bassinet. However, these seats were the only seats on the plane that did not have folding armrests, so Katie could not lie down to sleep. After we took off, however, we noticed empty seats behind us, so Jim and Katie took advantage of those to get some sleep. However, only 15 minutes into the flight, we discovered that our seats were right behind the smoking area curtain. In the expected French style, about half of the passengers smoked. Instead of being cleared by the plane's ventilation system, the smoke and odors seeped out the curtain right into our faces. Not a very bright idea, we thought, for an airline to design the seats for families with babies there.

Katie fell asleep right away, exhausted. But she woke up later and cried for a good while as we tried to comfort her. She finally slept four more hours. Jim and I only got two, and it was abysmal sleep. We were drained when we got to Paris around 11 a.m.

After we freshened up and got some much-needed sleep in a hotel during our layover, we mistakenly got on the wrong bus and went to the wrong terminal. Moving our small children and multiple bags at the speed required to fix such an error and get on the right bus was next to impossible. We made it in time, but just barely. As we waited to board the next flight, Joshua messed his diaper and got fussy, crying inconsolably. All the passengers waiting to board the plane looked at us with that "Oh great, their baby is going to cry throughout the whole flight" look. He finally fell asleep right before we boarded. We boarded about 45 minutes late, so our departure was delayed.

By the time we landed in West Africa, I had a splitting headache. We entered the chaos of the arrival terminal, pushing through the crowds and making our way through the passport police checks. We tried to avoid the constant bombardment of would-be baggage claim assistants who wanted to help us carry our luggage. By this time, the hot, muggy air was hitting us full force, and we were soon drenched in sweat. As usual, Africa welcomed us back with a bang. We also discovered that some of our luggage, including Katie's porta-crib, had not arrived.

After retrieving the bags that did make it, we waited patiently as the customs agents opened and inspected our luggage, looking for some excuse to detain us or ask for a bribe. Fortunately for us, the customs lady took a liking to Joshua – he charmed her enough that she waved us through without further hassles. Thankfully, Barb, Yolanda, and other colleagues were waiting to take us to the guesthouse. Finally, our traveling was behind us. Jim stayed behind with another colleague to take care of the missing baggage paperwork while the rest of us headed to the guesthouse.

We enjoyed a nice meal and some proper beds at the guesthouse. However, Katie had become so accustomed to sleeping in her now-missing porta-crib that she refused to sleep in the guesthouse crib and threw another tantrum. We finally dozed off to sleep hours later in the sweltering heat. Thankfully, the electricity came on long enough to run a fan.

Over the next week, we unpacked some of our things and got adjusted to the time zone. Both kids struggled to stay on a schedule, and we all struggled to sleep in the heat. We had brought over cloth diapers, not knowing whether we could find disposable ones. We spent many daytime hours preparing food and washing diapers and other clothes by hand. We survived nap time to nap time. By the sixth day, we were exhausted from the endless hand-washing of clothes and diapers and felt like we were getting nowhere. The kids were both screaming at one point, and we were undone.

Hot, tired, and sleep-deprived, I broke down and started crying. We felt like we were barely surviving and had accomplished so little. I asked myself, "What was I thinking? Why did I bring my family back to this place?" The lack of sleep and adjusting to our new norm contributed to my poor attitude. I struggled to see past that moment.

After two weeks, the lack of sleep and the heat had taken their toll on me. Our daily routine was just too exhausting. I became so ill that I visited a German doctor in town. She diagnosed me with anemia. We finally decided that the whole diaper thing was not worth our sanity. We abandoned cloth diapers and splurged on some disposables to make life more tolerable during our transition.

One day while still at the guest house during those first few weeks, our mission had hired welders to install some security grills over the guesthouse windows. Thieves had recently begun attacking the homes of foreigners in the city, and one of the other mission guesthouses had been targeted. On the day they were installing the security grills, Joshua developed an infected finger and began crying inconsolably. Katie became sympathetic and chimed right in with her baby brother, their cries harmonizing. We spent hours trying to comfort Joshua. No sooner had we succeeded at getting him to fall asleep than the welders began banging, grinding, and welding on the window above Joshua's crib. Sparks were flying perilously close to where he was sleeping. Jim yelled at the welders to stop, but they couldn't hear him through all the noise. When he shouted louder, Katie, who had also quieted down, began screaming again. It was almost comical, and we ended up laughing about it. Despite the challenges and chaos, we sat back and chose to be thankful for all God had brought us through.

We gradually adjusted to a new routine, and the kids began sleeping better. Katie started warming up to everyone and enjoyed all the attention. We made multiple trips to my former village home to move my things out and clean it up for return to its owner. Termites had done a number on all my stored belongings. They filled my oven, generator, and other items with termite tunnels made of damp mud, which rusted all the metal. Everything was covered in mildew and dust.

Katie quickly joined other children playing in the courtyard outside, laughing and playing in the dirt to her heart's content. We had a constant stream of visitors, some familiar and some not, wanting to see my new family. All the village women who came by to visit doted over Joshua. They were amazed at how fast I could ease him to sleep in the porta-crib, which had finally arrived.

With the recent unrest in the capital, we were anxious to leave the city and get on our way toward living "up country." We planned to move our belongings up to the town 8 hours north where we would be living. Afterward, we would travel six hours south to a village where we would spend two weeks in the home of some colleagues on home assignment. The goal was to practice "village living" on our own as part of our orientation back into the country, this time as a family. We felt it would be a piece of cake since we had both already experienced West African life and knew the ropes. We stocked up on food, diapers, and other supplies and headed up country.

This first trip did not go as we expected. It was dreadfully long, and the roads were winding and hilly. I got car sick, and Joshua was fussy. After we arrived in this unfamiliar town, we drove around in the dark for two hours, unable to decipher the odd directions we had been given to our destination. We finally found the home of the missionary family we would stay with, and at that moment, the rain began to pour down in torrents. Exhausted, we burst into their house, dripping wet, quite disheveled, with Joshua screaming. We must have been quite the sight.

After several days there, we took two days to travel the six hours south to where we would undergo our "village orientation." Katie was by now fed up spending days on the nauseating roads. She protested from her car seat, crying to get down. We determined that our main priority in life, after orientation, would be to get settled and avoid travel as much as possible while the kids were this young. Traveling with kids in Africa was a huge adjustment.

By the time we arrived at the village, we were fatigued. I was continually tired from the anemia and could barely move my back, which had begun to act up lately. Jim started running a fever and needed medicine. In addition, I needed a pain reliever. To our dismay, all our pills had spilled out during the trip and had gotten wet. So here we were, sick, without medicine, and out in the middle of nowhere. I've never taken a neighborhood drug store for granted since.

We knew several missionary families lived in another village about thirty minutes away, so we drove there. Thankfully, they had some

Tylenol. Despite this, Jim didn't get any better. Our new missionary friends drove him to the nearest large town to see a doctor, who diagnosed him with malaria. He started a treatment, which took several days to work.

Although Jim and I were not at our best during village orientation, Katie seemed to be in her element for the first day at least. She loved exploring the area around the house in this village, where several families had their huts. She ran after chickens, charmed the neighbors with her giggles, and "helped" the local women eat the peanuts they were pounding. She enjoyed them so much that she ended up getting sick. Within a couple of days, she and I were suffering from diarrhea, and I decided to treat us both with antibiotics.

Still exhausted, we ended our village orientation and traveled back to the coast for a team meeting. While there, another missionary family had to evacuate their daughter, Katie's age, to a nearby country by plane because she had developed cerebral malaria. This severe form of malaria impacts the brain and often leads to death. At one point, their daughter stopped breathing but did survive. This second-hand trauma shook me up quite a bit, knowing that this could happen to my children at any time. My fears about their safety intensified.

From then on, I treated our family for what I suspected any time we or the children ran a fever or had any other questionable symptoms. Thankfully, the medicines we needed were available in local pharmacies without a prescription, so we could stock up. If there was no way to get lab tests done, it was better to treat than wait until one of us became deathly ill. This proved an effective strategy, and the kids always got better quickly after treatment.

Over the next month, I continued to struggle with intestinal issues and general fatigue. Once again, sickness became a routine occurrence. By Thanksgiving, I had lost a considerable amount of weight. We had been living out of suitcases for three months, always traveling and constantly adjusting to changing surroundings, different food, lack of sleep, illness, and fatigue. All this stress impacted our physical and emotional well-being.

To add to it all, we had another long trip ahead of us: we had planned to spend Christmas with my brother and his wife, who now lived in the forest region where I had lived and worked 3–½ years prior. We broke the trip up into three days to be merciful to the children, and we stayed in the homes of other missionaries along the way. The roads had worsened in the past few years, so much so that I barely recognized them. We had a good visit, even though the trip was exhausting.

Besides illness and fatigue, Jim struggled with his own set of emotions. He was unaccustomed to hassles from police or soldiers, which were commonplace on road trips. Being ex-military, Jim took all of them as a personal affront and would typically brace himself for a conflict. One time an officer flagged us to slow down, approached our vehicle, and said something about the organization we served with and our paperwork. Jim misunderstood him and automatically assumed the officer wanted to hassle us about our permits, which had happened already on several occasions. I could see Jim's tension building.

When he reached into the glove box to get our papers, I stopped his hand and said, "Jim! Did you hear what he said? He said because he saw the name of our organization on the side of our vehicle, he already knows that our paperwork is all in order, so he doesn't need to look at it! He's letting us through!"

With a big sigh of relief, we continued our journey.

We were thankful when we could finally pack up all our things and move to the town up country where we would allocate. That town just happened to have a much cooler and more pleasant climate. We found a house to rent on the edge of town. It had a large, walled-in yard, its own well, electricity some of the time, tall pine trees for shade, and an annex for guest rooms, office, and storage. However, it needed a lot of repairs: the faucets, toilets, and roof all leaked. The cement walls were cracked, the windows had no screens, and it needed a paint job.

As we were busy making the house livable, Jim broke out with a case of boils that erupted on the end of his amputated leg. This made it impossible for him to walk for a month. I had to pick up the slack and do a lot of extra work while Jim grew discouraged by the day as the multiple courses of antibiotics failed to work.

With Jim out of commission and with a lot to do, we asked for help from colleagues and hired workers. Over the next few weeks, we had a constant stream of masons, painters, welders, carpenters, telephone repairmen, and electricians in our home. Our guard was tasked to clean out all the rocks and garbage from the sizeable yard. We also realized that if we hoped to survive with two small children, we would need to hire some house help. We hired a local woman, Fatu, who helped clean the house and wash dishes and laundry by hand. She even helped care for the children and cook delicious meals when we needed them.

A colleague helped Jim set up our solar panels. We hired a night guard to watch over our place, but he slept on the job continually. This made it hard for me to sleep, knowing we were vulnerable to thieves, an experience I did not wish to repeat.

It wasn't long before workers began to come in droves. One day a delivery truck arrived, dumping a whole pile of sand in our driveway for the masons. This blocked our vehicle from getting in or out. With Jim still feeling poorly, I had to direct all the workers, fix meals, nurse Joshua, entertain Katie, and tend to Jim's boils. I also traveled to town to find a telephone repairman to fix our phone line so we could send emails. We began running low on provisions, so I also made trips to the market. I tried to stock up on food and other supplies but could not find everything we needed.

While in the market, a crazy man began following me, pestering me constantly. When I asked standers-by to help me, they just laughed at me. This was the man's everyday behavior, and there were others like him. People in this culture allowed such individuals to roam, and they were not treated medically. The community simply tolerated them and their bizarre behavior.

In the market, I had difficulty finding anyone selling live chickens, the only chicken available. When I finally found a lady selling a rooster, she offered me an unfair price. I went ahead and paid it, too tired and weary to haggle. After placing the rooster in the back of the car, it left a special "present" on the floor. The cock then flapped around all the way home, spreading his little surprise far and wide inside the vehicle.

I couldn't find bread in the market, so I had to make some from scratch when I got home. Katie wanted to help, turning the whole ordeal into a long, drawn-out operation. She whined when she couldn't do it her way. Finally, the landlord arrived with his daughter, who took Katie off to play. Jim's boils had grown worse. He was in a lot of pain and started to feel depressed and helpless. Finally, after all the workers left, we ended our day with a time of prayer and worship, feeling a little refreshed in spirit afterward.

A few days later, the kids woke up early, both crying. I got them up, changed their diapers, dressed them, and prepared breakfast. Then I realized Jim was not himself. He was growing so depressed that he even shed a few tears, something I had rarely seen him do. I went to heat up some water to soak his leg, but I ran out of water because the water tower was empty. So, I went outside and hooked up the generator to pump water into the tower.

Then I noticed the night guard was using it all up, watering the garden. I ran over and told him to stop. He answered, "*D'accord,*" ("Okay," one of the few French words he knew), but he continued watering. He couldn't understand me despite my attempts and gestures to get him to stop.

Thankfully another worker who spoke French arrived and helped me communicate with our guard.

Running short on meat, I knew I needed more chickens, so I sent the worker to the market to buy some. He wanted me to go with him. So, after putting Joshua down for a nap, we drove to the market, taking Katie along. While in town, I stopped by the telephone office to see why they didn't come by days earlier when they said they would. They apologized, saying they would come that evening.

Arriving at the market, I searched for screws and anchors for our screen door. While waiting for one shopkeeper to go get some anchors, Katie was busily exploring the shop and spilled a container of hundreds of screws. I profusely apologized to the shopkeeper as we gathered up the screws one by one. As I met back up with the worker who had managed to find a few chickens, I stopped to buy some oranges, as well as some peanuts for Katie, who was becoming fussy. She immediately spilled half the peanuts on the ground and cried some more. After putting Katie in her car seat, she spilled more peanuts all over the car, making her even more upset. I tried not to lose my cool.

Back home, the workers helped me drill holes in the wood frames as we attempted to build the screen door together. Jim, who was feeling a little better, sat there coaching everybody. Unfortunately, the screws I bought were not the right size, so I had to return to the market to buy different ones.

After lunch, the guard slaughtered and cleaned the chickens while Fatu did our laundry and helped with some dishes. Jim started feeling well enough to take on some of the drilling himself. I got Joshua up from his nap and sat him down in his walker. Joshua then started to grab the drill bits. At that exact moment, Katie was in the other room, spilling the bag of oranges down the hallway.

After cleaning up that mess, I was getting very frustrated. I went back outside to help the guys only to notice that dark clouds began forming in the distance. We were concerned because there were still unsealed holes in the roof where Jim would mount the solar panels. I mentioned this to the head mason.

"Don't worry. It never rains in February," he reassured me in French.

Still doubtful, I ran to the storage room to find the tube of silicone that Jim had bought, only to learn that we didn't have a caulk gun. Jim and I tried to figure out how to get the stuff out of the tube by pushing and prying, with no luck.

The clouds grew more and more ominous, so I decided to leave nothing to chance. I sent our guard onto the roof with a tarp and some bricks to cover the holes. Unfortunately, the tarp wasn't large enough.

I turned to the head mason. "It sure does look like it's going to rain."

He shook his head again. "It never rains in February."

Just then, raindrops began to fall. I ran into the house, got some old plastic bags, and handed them to the guard, who used them to plug the holes. He raced down the ladder as the rain began to pour. I grabbed bowls and buckets out of the kitchen, and he climbed into the attic and set them under the holes to catch the water as the rain fell in torrents. I rushed back outside to shelter the generator because I had left it out in the rain. Of course, my feet got wet, so when I walked through the sawdust left by the men working on the door frames, I tracked it all over the house. Katie and Joshua immediately began playing in the mess, making it worse.

By this time, Jim was starting to get an attitude, and my own emotions were not far behind. We called it a day and sent the workers home. I still needed to cook the chickens, can them, heat up bathwater and give baths, fix dinner, and take care of Jim's leg. After dinner, just as I was preparing to wash the dishes, the landlord came for a visit. Exhausted and discouraged, Jim and I did our best to keep smiling and remain courteous and pleasant. We hoped he didn't ask about the holes in the roof. In the background, Joshua started screaming after Katie stepped on him (something she had started doing a lot lately).

After the landlord left, we realized that all the laundry was still on the clothesline, now soaking wet. Huge ants were now crawling all over the dirty dishes in the sink. Great! That night, like so many other nights during the past few months, we went to bed completely exhausted and feeling defeated.

The next morning, Jim started running a fever and having diarrhea. Would this endless cycle of one crisis after another ever end? We felt like we were constantly spinning our wheels, taking three steps forward and two steps back. Our morale was at an all-time low, and every day was a struggle. Every little interruption and setback discouraged us more. For the past several months, our letters back home to our prayer warriors, family, and friends were always full of crises for which we needed prayer.

Faithfully, our prayer warriors prayed. We learned that one church held a corporate time of prayer for us. Was this a spiritual battle, or were we just crazy for bringing our little family to this place and subjecting it to this host of insurmountable obstacles?

As Jim recovered, little by little, he was able to finish installing the solar panels and wire the house. He also put screens in all the windows and made other home improvements to make daily life more bearable.

The yard had potential with the beautiful shade trees, but it also needed a lot of attention. The previous owners had thrown their garbage everywhere. As the workers cleaned up, we discovered that the area we hoped to use as a garden had more trash buried in it, including an unusual amount of used flashlight batteries. We affectionately called the yard "the ancient battery burial ground."

Little by little, the yard began to take shape. I started planting flowers, vegetables, and fruit trees. Jim hung a few swings up for the kids. Our yard soon became a haven where the kids could play and where Jim and

I could retreat. We were super grateful to finally have a place of our own where we could begin to relax.

Part of settling into our new home was establishing new, structured routines. This helped our morale considerably. We began making a nightly habit of praying and worshipping together as a family, which was refreshing. Fatu, our house helper, was also a Godsend. With her help, we finally found time to start learning the local language. We knew it would take a couple of years to become fluent enough to tackle translation work. We hired language tutors who worked with us in formal sessions. We practiced what we learned as we visited neighbors, went to the market, and participated in the fledgling church that had formed in this town.

Having spent years in Africa already, I had always assumed that going to the market in our town and finding food and other supplies would be easy. I discovered this was not the case. We now lived among an ethnic group and culture which was exceedingly different from those I had worked with previously. Their unique language and customs gave me quite a bit of culture shock. Being a new mother of two also considerably reduced my reserve and energy levels.

Now, simple things like putting meat on the table seemed like insurmountable tasks. As my quest to find chickens in the market continued, I finally discovered the one area where most of the chickens were sold. In my past experiences, I could simply choose the chickens I wanted, haggle on the prices, and pay for them. But here, a barrage of women thrust their chickens in my face, yelling and carrying on, insisting that I buy their chickens. When I would look at one woman's chickens, the others would insult the first woman for butting in, then insult me for even thinking of buying that other woman's chickens and insist that I buy theirs instead.

Then, of course, there was also the language barrier thing. The cacophony of yelling and pushing women grew louder and more confusing until I finally broke down in tears and walked away with no chickens at all. I told Jim he would have to start doing the shopping if we were ever going to eat meat.

Jim later went to the market and found the "chicken ladies." As soon as they started their little ritual with him, he yelled at them, "Stop!" The women, who didn't speak English and were not sure what to make of this white man who yelled so loudly in public, instantly became quiet. In a commanding tone, Jim then proceeded to point out the chickens he wanted, haggle like a boss, and pay for the ones he chose. He then befriended an elderly lady nearby, called her "Mom," and from then on, he negotiated through her.

Every time thereafter, when Jim came to buy chickens, it was like the waters parted for him. He would greet and chat with "Mom," and she would hand-pick the ladies that brought their chickens for Jim to choose. And just like that, buying chickens became a simple matter. He will tell you that shopping in an African market can be stressful, even if it has a measure of adventure to it. I was grateful not to deal with all that added stress. Shopping meant carrying buckets and buckets of supplies and groceries to the car, which aggravated my growing back problems.

Chapter Ten

A FRESH START

O ur first six months as a family in Africa seemed like a blur. Jim and I had navigated many challenges and survived. Now that we were somewhat settled, things began going more smoothly. We had a few illnesses, such as Joshua contracting measles, and we all experienced occasional fevers, colds, mystery rashes, and gut issues. All four of us continued to struggle with malaria, but the newer malaria medications seemed to be working well. I continued to treat the illnesses at the first sign of symptoms, determined not to relive the nightmare that our colleagues had experienced with their daughter.

We gradually began enjoying our lives in our new home. We experienced occasional stresses, hassles, and frustrations with living cross-culturally, but things got easier for the most part. We focused more on ministry, language learning, working with the small local church, and establishing community relationships. God brought many ministry opportunities our way, and we began to feel a greater sense of purpose and accomplishment. I started treating patients from the neighborhood on our front porch.

God blessed us with other missionaries, foreigners, and Africans with whom we developed good friendships. Every Friday evening, we would worship and fellowship with missionaries in town. We shared a meal together and prayed with one another about whatever struggles we were encountering.

We created a small guesthouse in our annex building. I enjoyed hosting people traveling through the area, craving fellowship and friendship. We sometimes took visitors on outings to a nearby lake, canyon, or waterfall to enjoy nature's beauty. We avoided long trips as a family as much as possible and tried to stick to our routines which provided stability.

I felt safe most of the time, especially when I was home. Our home became a safe haven, and my garden became a great source of stress relief. I started collecting wild orchids, flowers, and other tropical plants on our nature walks and outings, as well as from neighbors and other expatriates. Before long, our yard became a miniature tropical paradise. I jokingly called my garden "my Prozac."

The children moved through developmental milestones, began playing together well, and seemed generally happy, with one exception. When Katie turned two years old, we noticed her behavior starting to change. Previously, she was always very friendly with strangers and enjoyed the attention of others. Suddenly, she showed extreme fear around anyone outside of our immediate family. When any colleague would come to the house, Katie would run and hide. Even when friends with whom she previously felt comfortable would visit, she would now act fearful of them, sometimes even screaming and crying. She would cling to me and bury her head in my chest as I tried to comfort her. She often woke up in the middle of the night screaming, saying she was scared.

Something was clearly going on with Katie, but we couldn't figure it out. Was it the malaria-prevention medication she was taking? This drug was known to cause bad dreams and even mental illness. Or did something happen to her that we did not know about? She had never been out of our sight for more than a few moments. We could only imagine that she was going through a phase, or perhaps the past year's stress and change had impacted her somehow. Maybe she was developing a shy personality like I had as a child. It seemed ironic that it started after our lives began to take on some "normalcy." Gradually, as Katie got to know people, she warmed up to them. However, she continued to struggle with social anxiety for years to come.

One day when Jim and I were in our car in the market, we witnessed a motorcycle accident. A man was riding his motorcycle with his wife and small child. None of them were wearing helmets. He lost control as they came down the hill near where we were parked. We watched in horror as his motorcycle plummeted into a meter-deep drainage ditch, and all three of them were thrown headfirst against the concrete wall of the trench.

We rushed to help them, loaded them into our car, and took them to the hospital. Miraculously, none of them had any serious injuries. We paid their hospital bill and took them home to their village, about 30 kilometers (18 miles) away. The villagers there greeted us warmly. This was the beginning of a lasting friendship with the people of that village, whom we visited regularly.

About a year after we arrived back in West Africa, we were settled in our new home and had become quite attached to it. We were progressing well in language learning and were fully engaged in the language project. Then we were hit with a huge emotional blow. Tensions concerning our project assignment arose with a colleague from another organization.

These tensions continued for the next two years. They weighed heavily on our minds, discouraged us, and made concentrating on language learning and ministry difficult. We began wondering if we had made the right choice in accepting this assignment. We even entertained the thought of starting over somewhere else. However, with the persistent encouragement of many colleagues, who had become dear friends, we pressed forward.

Additionally, we found ourselves repeatedly tricked or conned by local people. Many West Africans presumed Americans to be rich, and they were not entirely mistaken according to their standards. This made us a target.

One day a man came by our house saying he was one of our neighbors. He asked us to share with the neighborhood in slaughtering a cow. We just needed to give him some money to cover our part of the expense and a receptacle to carry back our portion of the meat. He said he would then bring it to us. Wanting to be neighborly, we gave him the money and a new basket we had just bought. He never returned. After inquiring with our neighbors, we discovered that we had been conned.

Another time, we helped a one-legged beggar to get a new leg. We paid his expense to travel to a mission hospital in the southern part of the country for surgery. There, he would be fitted with a prosthetic leg and do therapy to walk again. This way, he could get his mobility back and earn a living. We sent him by taxi. But a few months later, we found him in the market, still crippled and begging.

Other people continually came to our door asking for money to solve their crises. Even though I had experienced beggars and people asking for money during my previous single days in West Africa, I had never experienced them to this degree. Guilt from our privileged position as Westerners made us fall for their sad stories all too often. We found so many stories had been fabricated that it became hard to know whom to trust. We soon learned that this people group had a notorious reputation for deception and treachery. They seemed to esteem these character traits as virtues, although they gave lip service to honesty. We slowly became compassion fatigued.

As a matter of routine, most of our West African teams communicated at a daily scheduled radio time via long-range ham radios to send and receive messages. The country's presidential elections took place a little over a year after our arrival. A considerable increase in riots and violent demonstrations surrounded the election. One day during a radio session, the US Embassy announced that they were putting American citizens on high alert, recommending we prepare for a possible evacuation. Like other organizations, PBT advised its members to stock up on enough food and supplies to last at least a month and to get all our affairs in order. They even suggested we have our essential papers ready and pack a get-away bag just in case.

We had been through many contingency planning meetings to prepare for events like this, but now the likelihood of needing to evacuate was imminent. We made the necessary preparations and tuned in to the secure radio channel twice daily for updates from the Embassy. Amid all the chaos, the child of another American family we worked with became seriously ill, requiring a coordinated team effort to carry out an emergency medical intervention. The stress of this "close call" caused secondary trauma to me and others involved. This only increased my sense of insecurity in a country with poor medical infrastructure.

At about that same time, my brother, his wife, and another family traveled to a neighboring country for a vacation together. When the political tensions in our host country mounted, the borders closed. The couples were stuck on the other side of the border, unable to return home. So, they decided to enjoy a nearby tourist site with a waterfall, the same place near the war zone that I visited six years earlier. While at this tourist site, armed men approached my brother, his wife, and the other Americans with them. They marched the group at gunpoint into the forest while another man plundered their vehicles. At one point, one of the bandits fired a shot at one of the Americans in the group. Miraculously, no one was harmed.

My brother's group eventually freed themselves from the situation when they successfully overcame the man with the gun and confiscated his weapon. He and the other bandit ran off. Although God had once again delivered them from danger, the fact that such traumatic events took place in that part of the world was unnerving. Fearful thoughts dominated my mind. I couldn't shake the "what ifs" in this and other situations. What if they had been killed? What if that had happened to us? What if...? Just living in this part of the world was risky. Being foreigners made us targets. It seemed like only a matter of time before something like this happened to us. Secondary trauma and my imagination were beginning to wear away at my sense of peace.

A few weeks after the elections, more unrest exploded between two ethnic groups in our town. Constant gunfire passed very close to our house for about three hours. There was a strong military presence in town for the next couple of days. Most of the shops were closed. This would happen periodically in the years to come. We learned to stay inside the house to avoid any stray bullets coming over our wall and lay low until things passed.

In early 1999, the mild stomach pain I experienced on and off for years worsened. I also discovered a suspicious lump. In addition, Jim had been suffering from an infected toe for seven months and now developed boils again on his amputated leg. Since we had to travel to the capital for meetings, we took the opportunity to visit a German doctor. Unfortunately, the recommended treatment for Jim's toe didn't work, and his boils got worse. After we returned home, he became unable to walk once again.

As before, his morale declined, and I picked up the slack with everything else. Gradually, his leg infection spread to the other leg. Before long, his whole "good" leg was turning red. The antibiotics he had been taking were not working. Very concerned, we wrote home, asking for prayers. A colleague, who was a doctor, suggested a new generation of antibiotics. Unfortunately, it was unavailable in this country.

We wondered how we could get our hands on this much-needed medication when a colleague in a nearby town heard about Jim's condition in one of the ham radio sessions. He just so happened to have brought some of that medicine from the US and sent it up to us by courier. After Jim started on the antibiotics, the infection began clearing up immediately. A new clinic in the capital also opened with a surgeon who operated on Jim's foot, helping it to heal more quickly. We were relieved and thankful for these answers to prayer.

However, my stomach pain was still growing worse. This coincided with both kids coming down with fevers and Jim starting to feel ill again. We decided to take a second trip to the new clinic in the capital to seek medical help. There we learned that Joshua was anemic, indicating he likely suffered from malaria. Jim and the kids were treated for each of their ailments. One of the doctors at the clinic scheduled me for an endoscopy. I was surprised they could do this procedure at this clinic.

On the day of the endoscopy, Jim and the kids came with me to the clinic. The doctor told me he had never used his brand-new endoscope machine before. I was concerned that the device was in his office instead of a procedural suite, but I agreed to continue. He had me drink some numbing medicine and lay on the table. Then, without any sedation or assistance, he tried to put the scope down my throat with my husband and kids looking on. It was very uncomfortable. Before long, I was gagging and choking, struggling to get air. I began writhing on the table and flailing my arms, trying to signal to him that I couldn't breathe, but he ignored me.

Finally, I grabbed the tube, made a pulling motion, and began moaning through my nose in panic. When the doctor realized what I was trying to communicate, he pulled out the tube.

"Okay, okay, I have seen all I needed to see."

I looked up at him in disbelief, "What?" I sat up, catching my breath.

"Oh yes. Your exam is complete. Your stomach looks fine; there is absolutely nothing abnormal," he said with confidence.

"But my doctors in the US saw the ulcer with *their* endoscopic equipment," I reminded him.

"Your previous doctors must have misdiagnosed it," he said. "I believe that your problem must really be with your pancreas."

He ran some blood tests, but they all came back normal. I cautiously reserved judgment about his "diagnosis."

While at this same clinic, I visited a gynecologist for another pesky problem. After the exam, the doctor said, "Your condition is very concerning. You need a hysterectomy."

I grew skeptical.

The doctor continued his professional tone, "I will gladly perform the surgery myself at this very clinic."

"I don't think so," I thought to myself. I was now overly suspicious about submitting myself to another procedure at this hospital, as their practices began to appear as borderline quackery. We prayed about what we should do with this information.

Additionally, Joshua needed minor surgery, so we began looking for someone in West Africa who could do this procedure. We soon learned of a more reputable hospital with a pediatric surgeon in Abidjan, Ivory Coast, so we scheduled a trip there for Joshua and me.

We were thankful Josh and I could stay with some American friends, Wayne and Greta, while in Abidjan. We saw the pediatrician at the hospital and scheduled Joshua's surgery. While there, I also had the doctors investigate some of my health issues.

While in Abidjan, our American friends took me to a grocery store to get supplies. Abidjan sported beautiful, six-lane highways through and around the city, and modern buildings and skyscrapers dotted the skyline. The streets had signs and were well-paved. The lawns were manicured and beautifully landscaped. There was even a shopping mall and an ice skating rink. People actually stood in line at the bus stop. I almost cried getting groceries. It had been so long since I had been in a modern grocery store. There were abundant fruits, vegetables, meats, packaged foods, and choices! Everything was so clean! I almost felt like I wasn't in Africa, at least the Africa I had come to know.

Finally, the day of Joshua's surgery arrived. After they took him to his procedure, I sat alone in his empty hospital room. Once again, my mind wandered to everything that could go wrong, and I started worrying. Thankfully, my friend, Greta, came and sat with me and prayed with me, helping to pass the time. Joshua's surgery was successful, and I spent several days with him in the hospital.

The day after his surgery, I was scheduled for my own minor procedure. An ultrasound revealed that the lump was likely benign. However, I had a suspicious-looking growth in my abdomen. The doctor took a biopsy, which made me feel so dizzy I almost passed out. I was so grateful for Wayne and Greta's friends who visited us, most of whom I didn't know. Tears welled up in my eyes. The whole two days were beyond stressful. But God brought us through it and brought new friends to walk through it with us.

My biopsy results came back, telling us that the growth was benign but had the potential to turn cancerous. We were unsure what to do about it and if we could trust the doctors in our part of West Africa. Jim and I began corresponding by email with a doctor recommended by a friend in St. Louis. The pediatric surgeon also told us that Joshua would probably need a second surgery. Additionally, Jim was having problems with his prosthetic leg. He knew he would soon need to be fitted for a new one.

Our medical concerns were mounting, and there were timing issues with the translation project. We decided to return to the US for an early home assignment where we could get the healthcare we needed and where Jim would start working on a graduate degree. That decision came with mixed feelings. We had finally found a home where we could feel settled. Our ministry was just beginning to bloom. Our family had been in West Africa less than two years, yet here we were, already going back.

In some ways, I felt like we were giving in to defeat. The timing seemed wrong for ministry reasons, but we did need to deal with the medical issues. We would go in faith that God would lead us. He had a bigger plan.

We arrived back in the US in late July. But Africa couldn't let us go without leaving its mark on us: fresh boils erupted on Jim's leg just as we stepped off the transatlantic flight. We also were discouraged to learn that while we were in Africa, there had been a lot of turmoil in our home church. It had resulted in a church split, but no one had informed us.

When we left two years earlier, we had worked hard to raise up a thriving prayer ministry in that church. Prayer is not only vital to the church's spiritual health and growth, but we also counted on that prayer to sustain us in the spiritual battle we faced in West Africa. Now, that prayer offensive seemed to have all but unraveled. We wondered if this breakdown may have contributed to our struggles overseas.

Jim and I needed time to regroup and get solutions for our growing list of health concerns. Joshua saw a specialist who said he wouldn't need further surgery. I had surgery to remove the lump. Doctors ran more tests on my abdominal tumor, deciding to watch it closely. They found a second, smaller one and removed it. I had a repeat endoscopy, revealing my stomach was indeed inflamed. This convinced us that the physician I had seen in Africa was incompetent.

I was put on medication and started to feel better. As for Jim, his boils disappeared after a course of the proper antibiotics. He later got a new prosthetic leg. Then we moved into an apartment in Lincoln, Illinois, where Jim began attending seminary.

For the next nine months, I stayed home with the kids while Jim attended classes. We adjusted reasonably well. Joshua went through the "terrible twos," and we realized how spoiled he had become in the hands of Fatu in Africa, who always gave in to his protests and tantrums. We knew we had a lot of retraining to do, and we determined we would not have a nanny when we returned to West Africa the following year. Katie turned three and started learning to read.

I had moments where I struggled with depression, but for the most part, I kept myself busy with family responsibilities. I made new friends and got involved with the local church. I considered taking classes myself and finishing my master's degree. I had only one class left and a half-written thesis to finish that I had abandoned four years ago when Jim and I decided to get married. However, I decided against it so I could focus on spending time with the kids.

Overall, our home assignment was a refreshing time for us. It afforded our family the time to be "normal" for a while. We were able to get away from the chaos and stress of living in Africa. We took several regular vacations and reconnected with many friends and family all over the country. It truly blessed us. After nine months, our health improved, and our spirits were lifted. We recruited a new army of prayer warriors and purchased supplies to make our overseas lives easier. We were ready to return to our West African home as soon as Jim finished his classes.

Chapter Eleven

BEGINNING ONCE AGAIN

Returning for my third term in Africa was a much smoother transition than the previous one. We had already established our home. After about a week of unpacking, sweeping the dust, cobwebs, bugs, and rat droppings out of everywhere, and deep cleaning the house, we settled back in nicely. The kids, now three and four years old, remembered our home. They quickly jumped back into their old routines, rediscovered all their old toys, and enthusiastically played with their African friends.

We quickly refreshed our knowledge of the local language, and I began treating patients. Jim started comprehension checking the Scriptures our predecessor had translated into the local language. My garden had flourished while I was gone. Dozens of varieties of orchids and flowers were in bloom. We also had a wide variety of ripe fruit ready to pick: guavas, mangos, papayas, bananas, pineapples, strawberries, passion fruit, avocados, lemons, oranges, and grapefruit. We began enjoying the fruit of our initial labors in many ways.

We soon learned several missionary families were moving to our town or nearby towns. Several had children close in age to Katie and Joshua. Jim and I quickly formed friendships with them. We met regularly to go on outings, pray, and worship together, and we created a strong support system.

A few months after returning to our West Africa home, the long-standing civil war from a neighboring country began spilling across the border into our host country. Several families in our team had to evacuate from the affected region and relocate to safer areas. Rebel soldiers held a few missionary families, who lived in one of the border towns, hostage. The country's refugees were being rounded up, mistreated, and deported. Villagers along border towns were migrating en masse to other parts of the country. Fuel prices began rising, and people started protesting.

A week later, more locations along the border were affected. More missionary families had to leave for their safety. One family came and took refuge in our home for a short time while deciding what to do. United Nations workers, Peace Corps, and other aid organizations began pulling out. As tensions rose again, one of our US colleagues began perusing the Internet for news stories from the war front. She offered to send news highlights to any expatriates who wanted them. Anxious to stay abreast of developments, we began receiving and reading the daily updates.

Each day we read the latest war reports. Towns where some of our colleagues had lived were now under attack. Many people were killed, whole villages were ransacked, and people went missing. Some of our colleagues' African friends were murdered. Rebels raided a village where I had stayed for several weeks years ago to conduct literacy training, and people were massacred. Images of the people I knew from that village haunted my mind. Were they among those killed? I had no way of knowing.

The region where the language group that Jim and I had considered working in three years ago was now completely taken over by rebel soldiers. Many villages were brutally attacked. We shuddered to think what might have been our fate had we gone there instead. Rumors spread that the rebels wanted to overthrow our host country's government.

An insidious fear slowly began to fill everyone's hearts and minds, both Africans and foreigners alike. We were all on high alert. At one point, the rebel activity came within three hours of our home. Once again, we readied ourselves for a possible evacuation.

About a month into the unrest, a piece of my tooth broke off, and I began having severe tooth and jaw pain. The pain only worsened despite taking antibiotics and anti-inflammatory medications, so we traveled to the capital to find a dentist. Unfortunately, he could only complete half of the root canal procedure and told me I would have to return in a few days for the rest of the treatment. On the second visit, he drilled the tooth a second time, this time without numbing the gums. I could feel everything. He also cleaned my teeth with some saltwater solution. By the time he finished, my whole mouth was bleeding and swollen. I left in an emotional state of shock.

The next morning, my head was pounding. The whole side of my face was beginning to swell. I went back to the dentist and insisted something else was wrong. I finally convinced him to X-ray both sides of my mouth. After examining the X-rays, he apologized. I was right, he said; I did, in fact, have a bigger problem. The wisdom tooth was pressing in on the root he had just drilled, killing the tooth. In fact, he said, all my wisdom teeth were doing the same thing. He offered to have a surgeon friend remove them for me at a local hospital.

By now, I didn't trust any doctors at the local hospitals. A growing number of our expatriate colleagues had bad experiences too. That same week, another American had to receive a blood transfusion after almost bleeding to death from a botched C-section. I was determined not to have any surgery done locally. We drove eight hours up country back to our home and began making plans for me to return to the US to have my wisdom teeth removed. Meanwhile, I remained in a lot of pain.

We finally arranged for me to ride back to the capital with a colleague and then catch a flight to the US. After 16 long hours, 19 police checkpoints, where passengers were all interrogated to see if they were rebels, and other passengers in the vehicle repeatedly losing their lunch from the hilly, curvy roads, we finally arrived. My head pounded, and my jaw throbbed the whole time. Seven days later, still in pain, I finally flew out and arrived in St. Louis. I had the root canal redone, and the next day had oral surgery to remove all my wisdom teeth.

Within days of the surgery, the pain continued to worsen. My face was more swollen than ever. On my return visit to the oral surgeon, he revealed that I had developed dry sockets. I made several repeat trips over the next week to change the packing. After being in the US for nearly a month, I finally flew back home to West Africa. Then a second jaw infection developed. Two months after the whole ordeal started, and another round of antibiotics, I was finally pain-free.

Being apart from Jim and the kids for over a month was difficult for all of us. I struggled to keep up my courage and morale the whole time. I was in so much pain, alone without my family, and there seemed to be no end in sight. There were many moments of tears and depressed thoughts. However, daily emails and pictures from Jim and the kids kept me going. Jim reported that Joshua asked him one day, "Daddy, when Mommy comes back, will she hold me?" He reassured him that I would. When I returned, however, Joshua was very clingy and would get terribly upset whenever I left him alone, even for a moment. But he refused to let me hug him or kiss him goodnight at bedtime, and he would turn away from me. This went on for about six months. It broke my heart every time.

As we tried to get our lives back into a regular routine, we realized we were not alone in our struggles and discouragement. Many West African believers in our host country's churches were abandoning their faith.

Many colleagues we talked to faced discouragement, illnesses, loss of vision and direction, and loss of hope. There was a real sense of deep spiritual oppression.

So, as the war continued to rage along the geographical borders, Satan was waging another war on the spiritual front. I found myself questioning what purpose God had in all the trials he had put us through. They seemed pointless. Sometimes I cried tears so forcefully that I thought my head would split. Yet, through all of it, I chose to continue to trust him. I believed his reason would be revealed to me someday, even though the waiting was frustrating and discouraging. As for our translation work, we continued to plow forward. We chose to be thankful for God's daily sustaining grace and for the privilege to serve him each day we were given.

Chapter Twelve

I WON'T BE SHAKEN

E arly in 2001, we traveled to the capital city on the coast so our organization's translators, all men at the time, could spend the week away at a translation workshop. The wives chose to stay in the guesthouse with the kids for a time of fellowship, R&R, and shopping. One afternoon before the men left, I decided to take Katie along for a visit to a missionary friend, Debbie, who was an avid gardener like me. Gardening had become God's gift to help me cope with stress, especially that of living in a difficult place like West Africa. I enjoyed swapping cuttings of tropical plants, sharing ideas, and just hanging out with my friend.

While there, she told me about one of her African lady friends. Debbie had recently helped her landscape her yard, so she invited me to come and meet her friend and see the yard. I enthusiastically agreed. Soon Debbie, Katie, and I were driving down her neighborhood's bumpy, boulder-ridden back roads to visit her friend.

Once we arrived on the paved road, we saw something was wrong. A mob was running in our direction from further down the road in front of us. A large pillar of black smoke loomed behind them. I knew right away this wasn't good. We pulled over to the side of the road, rolled down the window, and motioned to a man running past our car. We asked him what was happening. He cried out in a panicked voice, "The rebels are taking the city! The rebels are taking the city!"

Panic kicked us into gear. We quickly turned the car around and headed back to Debbie's house. My heart was racing, and my head was pounding. Unimaginable thoughts were filling my mind. My chest tightened, and I found it hard to breathe. We barely made it back to Debbie's courtyard when we heard and felt the percussive booms of explosions in rapid succession. As we exited the car, I could feel every blast vibrating deep inside my chest, and I watched in disbelief as my hair and skirt jerked with each sound wave. The explosions were close.

I ran with Katie into the house and sat her on Debbie's couch. Within seconds, I watched the couch holding Katie jump off the floor from the vibrations of an explosion. Then, little chunks of the ceiling began falling onto the couch. Hundreds of people fled past the front gate to get out of town. Some didn't even have their shoes.

We got on the CB radio to call the guesthouse where my husband and other colleagues were staying. While listening, a driver for one of the local non-governmental organizations (NGOs) came on his radio, "They are attacking my vehicle!" We all were horrified, imagining the chaos unfolding before his eyes.

At that point, I was gripped with fear. All I could think of were the myriad horrors I had read about over the past nine months from the war front: brutal massacres of whole villages and other atrocities carried out by rebel soldiers. The thought that these very evil men could now be here in this same city as we were terrified me. As far as I knew, Jim and our son, Joshua, were at the guesthouse. Had the rebels made it to them? Were they in danger?

Fear overtook me as I imagined what could happen to them. There was nothing I could do to stop it. I trembled and fretted, feeling completely helpless and out of control. It was a full-blown panic attack. And then I saw Debbie.

She was out in her courtyard with the gate open, ushering frightened neighborhood children into her yard and sitting them in a circle on the ground. The kids were all crying, obviously very scared. But Debbie, calm in a way that was beyond my comprehension, sat down on the ground with them. She held their hands in a circle and prayed with them in a calm, controlled voice. I realized at that moment that whatever she had, I wanted it. Calm amid the storm and level-headed enough to recognize the most important thing to do at that moment.

Christian author Max Lucado talks about contagiously calm people. He points out how the Apostle Paul, with a belief system as sturdy as a tent with iron poles, resolved to "rejoice in the Lord," even while imprisoned and with threats on every side. Lucado says God calls us not to a feeling but to a decision deeply rooted in confidence in God's power, his control, and the end of the story.[1] As the Apostle Paul told the Philippians, we should be anxious about nothing, but let our gentleness be evident to all.[2]

Debbie was one of those contagiously calm people, exhibiting a gentleness that reminded others that God was in control. Why couldn't I react like she did? The bombs continued to go off non-stop for two hours. We got in touch with Jim and our other colleagues by radio and made an evacuation plan. Everyone scrambled to gather up passports and important papers. We awaited orders from the US embassy.

Then about two hours into it, we learned that the whole thing was an accident. There were no rebels. There was no attack. In an attempt to move around some ammunition at the depot, military personnel accidentally triggered a chain reaction, setting off a series of explosions. It took hours to get it under control. What a relief. And what a lot of worry for nothing. I had let my fears completely take over my thinking. So had practically everyone in the city, apparently.

After this incident, I realized it was simply not helpful to know every-thing happening in the news. Learning about the dangers that were happening or that might happen only made me more likely to become paralyzed with fear. If I was to stay in West Africa and accomplish the work God set before me, I would need to stay focused on Jesus and my task. So from that day on, I vowed not to read the news updates on the war front.

Over the next few days, we heard that unexploded bombs were still lying in the streets. One Canadian family saw a missile explode when a vehicle struck it, throwing bodies in all directions. Witnessing this event traumatized them. When Jim and I ventured out to buy a few things the next day, we saw about a quarter mile of decimated buildings near the military camp where the bomb depot explosions had started. Dozens of people had been killed or wounded. Some houses were caved in completely, and trees were charred. People had gently piled unexploded missiles and grenades along the roadside so vehicles could pass by. What a bizarre scene!

The translators left for their conference that evening while the rest of us stayed in the guesthouse. We all needed a reprieve, and it was good to visit with one another, debrief, and recover from the weekend's events. However, our rest was short-lived. As we were all sitting around and chatting, we suddenly heard a loud truck horn honking, followed by a loud crash. One of the other nurses, Stevanie, and I ran out to see what happened. At the intersection at the end of our road, all we could see was a massive cloud of grey dust. The area would usually be full of people selling things. People, covered in a layer of white, slowly emerged from the dust cloud, many of them streaked with blood. It was surreal.

A truck hauling cement was barreling down the hill when its brakes failed. The driver had lost control, crashing into the group of vendors on the corner. The contents of the cement bags had flown everywhere and filled the air, covering everything with cement powder. One woman emerged, wailing and carrying a small bleeding child. We knew it was bad.

As the dust cleared, we could see people carrying off a man with a broken leg. Other badly wounded victims were carted off in taxis. We rounded up several men who were less seriously injured and escorted them back to the guesthouse. They were covered entirely in cement powder, and some were blinded by the powder in their eyes. Their injuries included concussions, lacerations, and other visible wounds.

We helped them clean up, dressed their wounds, gave them medicine, and watched them for signs of worsening symptoms. At one point, an older man looked as if he was going into shock. One man had a fractured arm, and another had a large traumatic wound to the kidney area, along with multiple lacerations. We sent another guy to the hospital to get stitches on his head.

After they left, we returned to the accident scene to see if there was anything else we could do. By then, hundreds of people had gathered, and traffic had been completely blocked off. We couldn't get close enough to see what needed to be done, so we just went back home. At least 10 people died, among them a woman selling things at a roadside stand, along with her little girl and baby.

As we were leaving, the gathered crowd suddenly began rushing madly away from the scene. We instinctively ran like mad away from the scene as well. When nothing transpired, we realized that it must have just been a momentary panic that reverberated through the crowd. Everyone, including us, was on edge from all the events that had transpired over the past few days. I was spent and had no reserve left. I soon developed a nasty headache and had difficulty sleeping for weeks afterward.

When the translation conference was over, our family was relieved to return to the familiar surroundings and relative safety of our town up country. Unfortunately, however, all four of us came down with malaria at the same time. We noticed this frequently happened after our trips to the hotter, more humid climate along the coast, where mosquitoes were more prevalent.

Within weeks of our return home, another stressful event occurred. A single Canadian colleague in our town was being stalked by a mentally ill young man who also had a drug problem. One night he broke into her house drunk, became violent, and threatened her. She called us for help. Jim and one of our African co-workers promptly went to her place, tied the man up, and took him to the police, who jailed him. Despite posting a guard outside her home, she couldn't sleep for many nights after that. Neither could I. I worried that the young man would retaliate toward Jim for turning him in to the police.

Chapter Thirteen

SEASONS OF OPPOSITION

Despite all the chaos and stress we had been through, we were determined to persevere and succeed at the task set before us. Over the next couple of years, we established good momentum in the translation work. We got a better grasp of the language, and both Jim and I were involved with the translation project. Jim and an African colleague we hired and trained began working together daily, rough drafting Old Testament portions. They also met with nearby villagers to comprehension-test New Testament portions that our predecessor had rough-drafted. I worked around eight hours a week with another African we hired. We reviewed the revised texts, double-checked for comprehension errors, and revised and expanded a dictionary and other materials in the local language.

Our routine gave us a lot of stability, and we made real progress even though we experienced constant, unexpected interruptions. In addition to this, I began homeschooling Katie and Joshua during the day. In the evening hours, I was available to address our neighborhood medical concerns. On weekends, we were typically exhausted from our rigorous work week. But we felt accomplished. We established the habit of retreating to a nearby lake every Friday for a picnic, fishing, and relaxing, which we all enjoyed immensely. We grew to love our home, and our lives continued to get easier. Jim built a tree house for the kids. Several neighbor kids routinely came to hang out with our kids in our yard.

In July of 2001, I came down with a fever and intestinal problems and became very weak. I was diagnosed with a type of amebic dysentery and was put on intravenous fluids, losing over 10 pounds. A local doctor treated me with a newer drug. It put my heart into an irregular rhythm for about five hours and gave me double vision. It took me quite a few weeks to regain my strength. Jim and our African co-translator also became ill with malaria once again.

On September 11, 2001, the kids were enjoying some free-time activity while I worked with a translation assistant in the office. Jim was outside repairing the pump in our well while listening to the BBC on our short-wave radio. As I walked outside during a break, he called me over to listen with him. The reporter had just announced that a plane had flown into one of the twin towers in New York City. Moments later, a second announcement came: another plane had just hit the second tower.

We drove to a small restaurant in town and joined a growing crowd watching the events unfold on their satellite TV. The footage showed the smoke billowing from the buildings. Before long, the first building collapsed, then the second one. We watched in disbelief. Everyone turned to us and gave us their condolences, knowing we were Americans. The whole thing seemed too bizarre to be true.

Over the next few days, as international airline travel screeched to a halt, an overwhelming sense of panic and dread came over me. We were stuck here. As comfortable as we had become in our home and our lives in Africa, the thought of being unable to leave, especially when the world was suddenly thrown into chaos, left me feeling terribly insecure. We knew that life in West Africa was unpredictable and sometimes down-right dangerous. But strangely, we now felt safer in West Africa than in the US. Still, I felt trapped.

At the same time, we knew the US would likely retaliate soon enough. Now the potential for us as Americans to become the target of terrorism seemed real because we were far from the "safety" of our home country. The US embassy issued a warning to American citizens living abroad to take extra precautions, remain aware of their surroundings, and take heightened measures of vigilance.

Amid all these world events, our children reminded us that life goes on. They were innocent and unaware of all the events taking place. In her first-grade geography lesson, Katie learned about some of the countries suspected in the terrorist attacks. How would I teach my first-grader about the world out there and make it relevant to her life? I could only tell her that people were lost without Jesus, and we needed to pray for them and for peace.

In early 2002, as the US retaliated overseas for the 9/11 attacks, many people in our host country were unhappy with the US military response. Anti-American sentiment was growing in our town. This became very real one day when I walked into a shop where a group of men had gathered. Their leader was giving a hate speech about Americans. Unlike many foreigners in the region, I understood the language. If he found that out, I feared I could be a target.

I retreated to a corner, hoping he wouldn't see me. But he did, and he called me into his conversation. Before long, I was trying to speak reason into the situation. But he continued to attack me verbally, blaming me for all the faults of white men throughout history, including slavery.

I managed to get out of the shop, but I felt attacked. I was fearful and never wanted to go to the market again. Little by little, we began to hear from other foreigners about their experiences of opposition to their work and presence in the country. One African guard was attacked and stabbed simply because he worked for an American. Later, a colleague who had come to help teach the missionary children in our town was almost run over by a motorcycle, whose driver shouted "American" at her in a hateful tone.

At about the same time, unrelated to the terrorist attacks, many foreigners living in the capital began experiencing break-ins by armed bandits. Some of our colleagues were harmed in heinous ways. One of these tragic events occurred while we were in the capital, making us feel vulnerable and anxious whenever traveling there.

Months later, a border country where many of our colleagues' children attended boarding school experienced a coup d'état in which rebel factions overthrew the government. At one point, the children were trapped inside the walls of the school compound for days while rebel bullets flew over the compound walls. They were eventually evacuated by the French military. The families whose children attended that school spent months getting them safely back home and enrolled in another school. A younger child of one of these families stayed with us for several days while the parents traveled out of the country to get their older children relocated to a new school.

This new sense of insecurity, coupled with hassles of government paperwork, auto repairs, pets dying, and more illnesses, continued to wear on us. My back and neck pain worsened, and daily tasks took longer than necessary. Loneliness and a vast array of other stresses seemed to bombard us non-stop. These combined factors again pushed me into another depression lasting several months. I was often tearful. I was impatient and angry with the children, which left me feeling like a failure as a parent, and even more depressed. Katie began having trouble sleeping. She would have bad dreams, would cry often, and became afraid to sleep alone. I wondered if she was picking up on our stress or the chaos, making me feel even more helpless.

Then one day, while working in the office on the translation checking, the young man we had hired as a language informant began touching me inappropriately. I left the office immediately, trying to keep my composure. I asked Jim to pay him and send him home without an explanation. After the worker left, I told Jim what had happened. He was furious with the young man. Thankfully, I waited to tell Jim until the young man had left. Otherwise, he might have harmed the offender physically out of anger. The whole incident made me feel cheap and dirty. It left me reeling for days, but Jim was great about it and very supportive. He helped me cope with my feelings of inadequacy and vulnerability.

I spent my evenings addressing our neighbors' medical needs. Other patients from all over town would also come to my make-shift clinic. I treated a constant stream of burn and wound patients and others with intestinal parasites, respiratory infections, or malaria. As in my previous experiences, many people came to me when they were already at death's door. Having to regularly make life-and-death decisions weighed heavily on me.

Still, we continued to press forward in our work. Working in my garden one day, I realized that gardening was a lot like the struggles we had faced for the past four years living in West Africa. I had obtained four grape vines some years earlier. I planted, fertilized, pruned, and started new cuttings from them. The first year a deer completely ate one vine to the ground in seconds. Termites killed two other vines. We had no rain for seven months every year. We had to water the plants carefully each day to keep them alive during the prolonged drought. Occasionally, a snail infestation would strip the leaves from the plants. We had to pick the snails off every morning. Then there were the caterpillars and grasshoppers. Despite the setbacks, I managed to keep one vine alive, learning how to adapt the care of the vines to this harsh environment.

Living in Africa was no different. We had to constantly learn and adapt to the harsh life to continue growing and producing fruit. The Apostle Paul's letter to the Galatians encouraged me: *"Let us not become weary in doing good, for at the proper time we will reap a harvest if we do not give up."* [1] We followed the words of Paul in his letter to the Ephesians: *"Therefore put on the full armor of God, so that when the day of evil comes,*

*you may be able to stand your ground, and after you have done everything,
to stand."* [2] We prayed, asked our prayer warriors back home to pray, and
continued pressing on. We waited patiently for God to bear fruit in our
ministry and trusted him to help us keep standing.

Four years into West African living as a family, we realized it would just
be tough. The easy life was a fantasy, not reality. We would have to slow
down and lower our expectations to survive the long haul. We continued
to honor our marriage covenant to pray daily together. The growing
team of missionaries in our town met weekly to join in corporate prayer,
worship, and fellowship.

Jim and I found moments of rest and pause as best we could throughout the week. We scheduled outings and little vacations with fellow
missionaries to scenic areas, which was always refreshing. We celebrated
holidays, birthdays, and other milestones with parties for the kids and
their friends to make life seem as enjoyable and "normal" as possible. In
the evenings, our little family would sometimes watch movies borrowed
from a fellow missionary couple, whose own family frequently sent them
over in care packages. We continued to retreat to the lake every weekend
and take the kids to a park-like area to ride their bikes. We got out in
the community and sat alongside our neighbors, chatting and letting the
kids play together. These were all enjoyable moments. By the end of that
year, I determined that I would spend more time with God and more
time resting to clear and focus my mind. This helped considerably.

By mid-2003, we had finished a provisional translation of the New
Testament in the language where we worked. We had completed a
three-year term, and our family was finally ready for another nine-month
US home assignment. We spent those nine months recharging ourselves
with travel to visit friends, family, and supporters. We also visited doctors
to address some of our ongoing medical issues. My doctors identified a
bulging disc in my back. I began physical therapy and learned how to do

daily preventive maintenance to manage the pain and reduce the risk of future injury as we looked ahead to returning to Africa. However, one radiological exam of my neck revealed another problem – my thyroid gland was enlarged.

Further tests revealed that I had several tumors on my thyroid gland. The biopsy showed they were benign for now but would have to be watched. We would have to find a way to follow up on this regularly if we returned to Africa.

The ongoing health issues that Jim and I faced kept us humble. They reminded us of our human limitations and made us rely more on God's grace and provision rather than our own strength. Although our home assignment had been refreshing, strangely enough, something inside made us all long to return to our African home. As our US time drew to a close, we prepared for another three-year term in Africa with anticipation.

Chapter Fourteen

CARRIED

As our flight landed back in West Africa, many of the passengers began to cheer. We found ourselves, our children included, joining them. As much as we had struggled in this place, it had become home, especially for our children. Katie and Joshua knew little else. After several days of buying supplies in the capital for the months ahead, we loaded up our vehicle and traveled back to our home up country. As we pulled into the gate, Joshua broke out in tears when he saw his dog, Sherman. The kids jumped out of the car with glee, reunited with their pets, toys, and the familiar surroundings of our home.

Settling in consumed our lives for the first week. In many ways, it felt like settling in for the first time. Once again, West Africa had taken over our house while we were gone. We spent days shoveling out dust, cobwebs, and the wasp and mice nests that had accumulated over the past nine months. A mouse had even built a nest inside one of Jim's guitars. All the clothes left hanging in the closets and every dish in the house had to be washed. We repainted the walls and deep-cleaned the grungy dust and mildew-covered shelves, furniture, rugs, and books. The termite-eaten furniture needed to be replaced, and the house's electrical system required maintenance. We hired workers to convert our garage into a school room and repair cracks in the walls. Jim installed new solar panels, and we unpacked all we had brought back. Jim and I triaged all the kids' toys and decided which ones would have to go to make room for the new ones. It was a purging but also a new beginning, both physically and symbolically.

We gradually adjusted to our new routine. Every morning at 6:45, our gray parrot, whom colleagues had cared for in our absence, sang his usual repertoire for us. We grew accustomed once again to the sounds of motorcycles, cars, roosters, bleating goats, children laughing in the distance, and the night crickets chirping. The familiar smells of cooking fires and local foods being prepared by our neighbors wafted back into our days. Over the next many months, we experienced a period of great productivity, good health, and joy in the Lord, despite all the daily grind stuff.

During the extreme heat and dry-season drought, we dusted the house daily. Then, when dry season gave way to the violent daily monsoon-type rains in the summer months, we switched to airing everything out to fight mildew growth with make-shift clotheslines strung everywhere inside the house. Each season had its all-too-familiar routine.

However, this year, 2003, our region experienced more rain than usual. The rivers, wells, and septic tanks overflowed and flooded. Soon, a typhoid epidemic broke out in our community. One American colleague and many African friends became ill.

I had recently flown to Dakar, Senegal, for further tests to monitor the tumors in my thyroid and my abdomen. Our attempts to find the needed testing closer to home failed. The doctor in Dakar said the tumor in my abdomen was growing and I would need surgery soon. Additionally, Jim had injured his shoulder. As the months went by, the pain became so intense that it limited his arm's use and mobility. We needed medical treatment that we could not get in West Africa. So, after being back in the country for only six months, our whole family flew back to the US for a month to get needed medical interventions once again.

Back in the US, Jim was relieved that his problem was only a "frozen shoulder," where scar tissue had sealed his joint tight. Jim took his physical therapy very seriously and restored the use of his arm within the month. Meanwhile, I had surgery to remove the growth in my abdomen.

A week after my surgery, I developed typhoid-like symptoms. The hospital re-admitted me for a three-day stay to treat me for suspected typhoid because of my recent exposure. After my second release from the hospital, we met with one of the top thyroid specialists in St. Louis. He would look at my biopsy results and get back to me.

As our month in the US ended, both Jim and I felt ready to return to West Africa. No news from the thyroid doctor seemed to be good news, so we got everything in order and returned to West Africa. About one month back in Africa, however, we received an email from the thyroid specialist. The tests had shown pre-cancerous lesions in my thyroid, which the previous lab had missed. The most prudent thing to do, he said, was to remove that part of my thyroid as soon as possible. The thought of yet another US trip in one year disheartened us. After much prayer and discussion, we decided to travel back to the US for the holidays and have the surgery done.

In the meantime, we focused on our work and were productive. Jim made great strides in the translation work. I continued to homeschool Katie and Joshua in the mornings, work on language materials in the afternoons, and treat patients in the evenings. We still had time to continue hosting visitors. I joined a mobile medical team in a remote location and helped treat over 1,000 patients in one week. We saw many open doors for ministry. Jim transitioned into a leadership role in PBT, necessitating visits to other teams in different regions of the country. Despite the toll the bad roads took on my back, we enjoyed the opportunity for fellowship with our colleagues.

Late in the fall, as the rains eased, stagnant water pooled, and the mosquito population increased, causing the number of malaria cases to rise. Our African co-translator and his two-year-old son both became ill. The boy's mother asked me to come by the house to see her son. I immediately noticed he was severely ill, lethargic, and barely conscious. His eyes drifted off with a rigid stare, a sign of possible cerebral malaria.

I obtained a blood sample and examined it under my microscope. This confirmed what I had suspected: with over 25% of his blood cells visibly infected, I knew he was suffering from a severe case of malaria. Within days he would likely lose 75% of his blood volume as the parasites multiplied and ruptured his blood cells. There was no telling how anemic he already was. He didn't have much time. I had one treatment left of a new anti-malarial drug known to work rapidly.

I crushed the pill, mixed it in some jelly, and prepared to give it to her son. He was listless, barely able to swallow or stay conscious enough to obey my commands. I wondered how I would get him to take the medicine. I held him, spooning the mixture into his mouth, but he spit it up over and over. His mother and I continued to scoop up his vomit, with the medicine in it, back into his mouth, hoping it would stay in his system long enough to absorb. I was determined this boy was not going to die on my watch. Finally, when it seemed like he was keeping it down, I went home. I tossed and turned and prayed all that night.

First thing in the morning, I went over to check on the boy. I was so relieved to see him sitting up, alert, and eating. His fever was down, and he even asked for more medicine, so I gave him the remainder of the treatment. A microscopic examination of his blood confirmed that the medication was working. Only 1 % of his blood was now infected. By the second day, there was no evidence of the parasite in his blood. He grew stronger each day, and we were thankful that God intervened and saved the boy's life. I was also very grateful we could get this new, life-saving medicine.

This and many other similar experiences gave me a greater burden for doing something more with the medical work. I decided to join more future medical outreach teams. I also began hearing of a region of the country that had been very closed to missionary work until now and felt a quiet stirring in my heart that perhaps God wanted me to be involved in reaching that area. I had no idea how, but I kept my mind and heart open for an opportunity.

As the time approached to fly home to the US for my surgery, I was torn. Our work had taken off, and so many good things were happening. Our family routine was comfortable, and the kids were thriving. The team we worked with in our town and region was a fine group. We all had tremendous momentum, energy, and excitement with everything God was doing. It was hard to leave at such a critical moment. But I trusted that God was in control and prayed that he would reveal his purpose in what we considered a "bump in the road."

The kids and I traveled back to the US together, and Jim joined us later. The surgeon removed half of my thyroid, and my recovery went smoothly. We had a good time visiting friends and family over the holidays. While in the US, a news story caught my eye, and I began feeling a tug on my heart to consider adopting a child. However, I kept this thought quiet for the time being.

Jim flew back to West Africa in early January. I followed with the kids several weeks later to give me adequate time to recover from the surgery. As was typical, our flight back to Africa involved three connecting flights: one from St. Louis to Chicago, one from Chicago to somewhere in Europe, and one from Europe to West Africa. We rarely had any complications with this itinerary. However, while the kids and I were on the plane in Chicago, ready to take off, there was a delay of more than two hours. The pilot spoke over the PA system, announcing that our departure would be delayed due to a "minor" maintenance problem. So, we waited for what seemed like an eternity.

Finally, the pilot spoke again, saying the plane's hydraulics were not working. I felt my anxiety slowly rising. I was always a bit nervous about flying, but I always reassured myself with the frequently quoted statistics about how safe flying was compared to driving a car. Sure, I had some bad experiences with certain African airlines and managed to avoid flying with them for quite some time. However, I had never encountered a plane with technical problems. I wondered why the crew didn't just get us off the plane. Other passengers wondered the same thing.

People became restless, murmuring and looking out the window for some sign of reassurance. Finally, three hours later, the pilot spoke again, telling us that they had fixed the problem, so we prepared to take off. However, I was still anxious, so I continued saying prayers for God's protection, as I often did whenever we took off on a flight.

As the plane took off, I noticed we weren't gaining altitude as we should. I had been on so many flights by this time in my life I knew this one felt different. Or was it just my anxiety getting the best of me? About four minutes into the flight, the pilot and the flight attendant spoke to the passengers again, announcing that we would be returning to Chicago. They said there was a "problem," and we couldn't fly this plane over the ocean. They didn't mention what the problem was, and no special instructions were given.

By now, about half the people on the plane were in a panic. Everything in me wanted to cry, but I did my best to hold back the tears and the look of fear in my eyes to avoid alarming the children. A man down the aisle from me began wiping the sweat off his brow, looking worried. An elderly French lady began breathing heavily, praying the rosary aloud in French.

As we approached the runway, I could see dozens of fire engines with lights and sirens blaring, racing along under us as we prepared to land.

Other passengers saw the same thing. I exchanged concerned looks with a man across the aisle. This only served to heighten our fears, and I became terrified at the possibility of a crash landing. Then, at the moment of impact, everyone held their breath.

Thankfully, we landed safely. Everyone was ecstatic and cheered. Then the passengers anxiously began getting out of their seats, wanting off the plane. The flight attendants urged everyone to sit back down and be calm. They then informed us that there had been a fuel leak, which is why they couldn't fly the plane, and that they would allow us to get off shortly.

We sat for a long time before the pilot spoke to us again about another problem: our flight was now considered an international arrival. Everyone on the plane, some of whom were not American citizens, would be unable to re-enter the US without security clearance. Passengers grew restless. I knew by now I would miss my connecting flight in Brussels. I had no idea what would happen next.

An hour later, all of us were still seated on the plane. The flight crew told us they believed the fuel leak had been fixed and hoped to take off again. At that point, all mayhem broke out. Some people began yelling at the flight attendants, demanding to let them off the plane. People were threatening to riot. Finally, faced with the angry crowds, the crew let everyone off the plane and allowed them to gather in a holding area.

Over the next four hours, disoriented crew members tried to appease the agitated crowd. I was weary and tired. The kids occupied themselves with their electronic games. We eventually stood in line with other passengers who were finally getting somewhere, securing flight changes, hotel and meal vouchers, and anything else they demanded. I managed to negotiate an airline change, but it would require a three-day stay in Chicago and a one-day stay in Paris. After much deliberation, I also got hotel and meal vouchers for three days. We would have to come back the next day to work out the details of the flight arrangements.

It was now about 1:30 a.m. We wandered for a long time in the airport, lost and trying to find our luggage to no avail. Then I had to find the airport shuttle to the hotel. After finally arriving at the hotel and getting the kids to sleep, I lost it. I had a meltdown, crying for a long time from exhaustion and the stress of the whole traumatic event. In those wee hours of the morning, I reached out and called one of our mission's member-care personnel. I needed to debrief.

Thankfully, our member-care person contacted members of a Chicago church. Over the next few days, those church members supplied us with winter clothes, snacks, and friends for the kids to pass the time. Their church even took a love offering to help pay for my extra expenses, such as the hotel I would have to pay for in Paris. Unfortunately, only half of our luggage was found. No one had any idea as to the whereabouts of the remaining bags.

Resting in the hotel over the next few days, I had time to reflect on all the events that had transpired. Despite all that had happened, I realized I had to be thankful for God's provision amid the chaos. Thankfulness, I had learned, helped put everything in perspective. I tried to think of anything I could be thankful for. I was grateful that the pilot had the wisdom to turn back and land the plane when he could. I was thankful for a safe landing and for a clean, warm (not to mention quite posh) hotel. I was grateful for airport shuttles in the winter cold, that the airline paid for our meals and rooms, and for the kind, accommodating hotel staff. I was thankful that the remaining flights were confirmed, and that the bags we did find had some clothes in them. And I was so grateful for the warm generosity of the Christian family who came and helped total strangers. My tears of frustration turned to tears of joy as I realized how God's loving hand was still caring for us in so many ways through this difficult experience. I made it a point to email all our prayer supporters to pray over the remaining trip.

One thing I did not expect was the impact this traumatic experience with flying would have on my brain, creating an added post-traumatic anxiety response every subsequent time I flew. In fact, I had to really calm myself before getting on the next plane. My mind struggled to cope with the now unpleasant reality that flying was a necessary part of living overseas. I already determined that I would never fly with that airline again. This was my mind's attempt to rationalize why the near disaster happened in the first place. I reasoned that future stress could be avoided by using a different, more reputable airline. I was also determined never to fly through Chicago again. And I never did. Not that that would necessarily have mattered. Eventually, even that seemingly rational decision to avoid potential danger would not eliminate my fear of flying from that point on.

As is common with PTSD, avoidance, bargaining, and stating absolutes seem like logical ways to cope with out-of-control situations. We go to extremes to avoid a similar situation so we don't get hurt. We perceive these strategies as a means of regaining control. The reality is that nothing is ever certain or really in our control. It would take me years to finally come to terms with the fact that only God's sovereignty is certain. Instead of trying to get control, I needed to surrender my control to God. I knew this in my head, but putting it into practice was a constant battle.

Chapter Fifteen

RESTLESS

In the months following my return to our West African home in early 2005, God continued to move in amazing ways in our ministry and the ministries of our regional colleagues. I joined several more medical teams in remote, unreached areas, and the translation work moved forward with significant progress. Spiritual doors in some regions that were closed for decades began to open. I started teaching a literacy class with some neighborhood women, giving me many opportunities to discuss spiritual things and address their needs more personally. At the same time, some Christians in the local church experienced severe persecution for their faith.

As we fellowshipped with other foreigners in our region, I noticed that our kids were the happiest when we had other children around, so I made it a point to create as many opportunities for them to socialize with peers as possible. I truly enjoyed entertaining guests and their children. I found myself wanting more family and less translation work. I wondered if God's purpose in leading me into translation work was so my husband, Jim, would eventually be empowered and enabled to do it. Jim needed a wife who would support him, help him when needed, and also keep the family happy and healthy. Although some may think of this as giving in to stereotypes, I began to feel differently. God had made us a team, and our roles changed and shifted to our natural abilities and giftedness over time. I welcomed a strong man in my life to take on responsibilities and leadership in our family and ministry that I had previously felt burdened to carry. I began to realize that all the education and accomplishments in the world paled compared to the satisfaction I found in just being home with my family, being a good mother and wife, and being a home-maker. Letting my husband take the lead benefited our whole family and strengthened our marriage. Though some women may have resented it, I did not. I felt blessed to have the choice.

One night I had a dream where I was on my deathbed, and many children were gathered around me. At that moment, nothing else I achieved in life mattered except my family, being a mother, and being called "blessed" by my children. My outlook had changed. Instead of aspiring to be a successful linguist, nurse, or missionary, I simply longed to be the best mother I could be. This was as much a calling on my life as anything else ever was or could be. My heroes were no longer the missionaries that I had idolized. Instead, they were the housewives, the mothers, the women right in my backyard who labored day after day in silence and in the absence of notoriety. I now saw these women to be making the biggest impact in the world, shaping and molding the hearts of their little ones to follow God's plan for them and to be pillars of strength in a fallen world. I counted it an honor to be in their ranks. I realized that I had learned more about life, patience, love, and all other virtues, living out my destiny as a wife and mother than I had in doing anything else. If I failed in these roles, I failed at everything.

Around the same time, one of my close friends working in a town near us had her fourth child. After seeing the baby, Joshua began longing for a "little brother." I grieved over the loss of my dream to have a large family. We had abandoned that dream ever since my doctor told me I was a high pregnancy risk and advised us against having any more children while in Africa. We had felt at the time that our ministry was our primary calling. Yet my desire for more children grew stronger, and I felt an emptiness inside. My son wanted a brother. My daughter, now almost eight years old, continued to struggle with being shy and connecting well with friends. Maybe a sister would help meet her social needs. I wrestled with the decisions we had made. Had I trusted God with everything, or had I given in to fear?

One day I sat looking at a portrait of our family and felt something was missing. I sensed it was incomplete – that more children belonged in that picture. Thoughts of adoption came to mind again. Would adoption be an option for our family? Jim and I had talked about adoption years ago, but we had not felt ready at that time. I decided to bring up the topic again one day on a long road trip. After eight hours of discussion, we decided we had more than enough room in our hearts to love another child or two.

We began exploring adoption options. Very few adoptions from the country we lived in were possible. We decided to find an American agency that would work with us while living overseas. After months of sending emails to the best Christian adoption agencies, we finally found one willing to work with us. We spent months filling out paperwork, getting police and FBI clearance, and trying to find a way to get a home study done in Africa. Because we lived overseas, our choices were limited. Finally, by early February 2006, we were approved to go through with the adoption. We began the formal process of adopting a one-year-old boy, Gabriel, and a three-year-old girl, Aisha, living in separate orphanages in Guatemala.

Chapter Sixteen

THE ACCIDENT

O ur translation project reached an exciting milestone in the spring of 2006. We had completed the New Testament translation and needed to conduct a final read-through with our co-translator. This would be at least a two-month process, so Andrea, the daughter of some friends back in the US, came to help tutor our children so I would be free to participate. We were thrilled to finally be at this final stage before sending the New Testament to the printer. We anticipated leaving for home assignment later that year once the adoptions were finalized. This would enable us to travel to Guatemala to pick up our children and bring them home. After Andrea arrived, our translation team made considerable progress in the final edits of the New Testament translation.

A colleague from a nearby town came to one of our Friday night gatherings. While there, she asked me if I could accompany her and her grandson on an outing to a nearby canyon with breathtaking views that colleagues had discovered several years prior. I knew the canyon well after taking dozens of visitors there over the past several years. I agreed to meet her and her grandson at a rendezvous point the following Saturday since she didn't have a phone.

I began to feel sick the following Friday evening before the scheduled outing. I was tired, my back was hurting, and I started having an ominous feeling about going the next day. I knew that the trip would be exhausting. It involved several hours of driving on bad roads and rigorous hiking in the unrelenting African heat. I had no way to contact my colleague about canceling. That night I agonized over it, feeling strongly that I shouldn't go. But I did not want to let my friend down, much less leave her and her grandson stranded at the rendezvous point after they had walked a good distance to get there. I had a sleepless, restless night.

Saturday morning came, and I mustered my strength and willpower to pack everything up for the outing. Our children's tutor, Andrea, decided to come along, as well as an African neighbor we hired to guard our vehicle while we were out exploring. We picked up our friend and her grandson and headed to the canyon. The hike went well, with only a few mishaps.

After dropping my friend and her grandson off around 5 p.m., I continued down the country road toward home. About eleven km (seven miles) outside the town, I was about to pass a group of women walking toward town when an eight-year-old girl suddenly ran from behind them into the road right in front of the car. I slammed on the brakes and swerved away, but the girl was running too fast. Despite my best efforts, it was impossible to avoid her. Witnesses and family said she was returning from a village on one side of the road to her village on the other side. Another witness said children were chasing her.

My heart froze as I heard the thud of her body against the right front corner of my vehicle. I threw the car into park, and we all ran out to see if she was okay. She lay moaning on her side with her scalp splayed open. I was horrified. The women who had been walking began wailing hysterically around us, and a crowd began to gather. I was shaking, afraid everyone would turn on us. I had heard of two other cases where foreigners had hit pedestrians. In both situations, the foreign driver was violently attacked or jailed. Just then, out of the crowd, one man, who appeared to be either crazy or slightly inebriated, told me repeatedly in the local language, "Everything is going to be okay, everything is going be okay."

Our African neighbor helped me put her in the back of our vehicle. I asked Andrea and our neighbor to sit with her, hold her head up, try to console her, and keep her alert. Quickly, I got in the driver's seat and drove the remaining 11 km to the town hospital. Barely able to control my shaking and rapid breathing, I felt like I would pass out as I drove. I began crying out to God under my breath, praying that she would be okay.

Our neighbor carried the girl into the emergency room as soon as we arrived. Right away, they began to clean and sew up her wounds. She also had a broken arm and was holding her side. Our African neighbor took Andrea back to our house. He informed Jim, who sent another colleague, JD, to the hospital to stay with me. Together, we laid hands on the child and prayed. The words of Jesus came to mind:

"I tell you the truth, you can say to this mountain, 'May you be lifted up and thrown into the sea,' and it will happen. But you must really believe it will happen and have no doubt in your heart. I tell you, you can pray for anything, and if you believe that you've received it, it will be yours." [1]

As we prayed for the girl, I believed the words of Jesus with all my heart – that God was going to save her. I wondered if this was the moment of truth where he would reveal himself to these people. I prayed that he would use her healing to bring glory to himself and bring this people group to salvation. Confidence and boldness filled me as I prayed like never before. I stood by the girl, holding her while they sewed up her head. The staff kept telling me she would be fine.

The girl's mother soon arrived at the hospital. She had a very grave look on her face. Despite my feeble words of sympathy and apology, I could do nothing to change her afflicted countenance. My own grief was bad enough; I could not imagine what she was going through. I thought of my own daughter, about the same age, and how I would feel if this had happened to her. The horror of the situation was beyond words.

While I sat beside her and her mother, waiting for an X-ray to be done, I rested my hand on the little girl's arm and felt her pulse. It was rapid, as was her respiratory rate. The X-ray revealed no skull fractures, and the staff continued telling us she would be fine. But I had a sinking feeling that she was in real danger, based on her vital signs. I prayed even harder. We offered to pay for her medical expenses. With the reassurance of the hospital staff, JD took me home. I tried to relax and calm myself, praying and repeating the hospital staff's reassurances in my mind. I firmly believed that the God of miracles would come through in this situation.

First thing in the morning, Jim took me to the hospital to check on the girl. She and her family were not there, so we asked the hospital staff where she was. A sinking feeling swept over me when nobody would give us a straight answer. I knew she was gone. Finally, after much prodding, a hospital staff member admitted that she had passed away around 9 p.m. the night before, and the family had returned to their village to bury her.

At that moment, I buried my head in Jim's chest and sobbed uncontrollably. My fervent prayers in faith had gone unanswered. And worse, I had killed someone. I felt myself falling into a very dark place, sensing God had completely abandoned me. I cried in that dark place for what seemed like an eternity.

The hospital staff stood there, staring quietly. Then, finally, several of them broke the silence and spoke up, encouraging us to go to the village and attend the funeral. They argued that the right thing to do was to offer our condolences to the family and help however we could. So, we left directly from the hospital and arrived in the village about 15 minutes later.

The village turned out to be a sister village to the one where we had helped the family who had been in the motorcycle accident eight years earlier. Since we had spent a lot of time establishing relationships there, we recognized some of the village elders who had gathered for the burial.

This gave us a little peace of mind, knowing there were familiar faces in the crowd. Jim was summoned to join the men while I was taken to where the women had gathered.

The crowd of women that had gathered there was significant. A sea of hundreds of women from that village and the surrounding villages were wailing and carrying on around the mother. The din of wailing voices increased as I was paraded through the center of the crowd toward the mother. She reached out to me and pulled my head toward her chest. Was this a gesture of camaraderie? Shared sorrow? Forgiveness? I wasn't sure what this meant. All I knew was that I was the object of everyone's attention. I felt incredibly vulnerable, as if I was on display in a mock trial. I could not hold back the tears and began weeping openly. Nothing in my life could have prepared me for this. I had never felt this humiliated and ashamed. It was more than I could bear. Like my childhood self, hiding in the clothes hamper, I wanted to crawl into a hole and hide, making it all go away. It was a very hard moment for me.

Whether out of embarrassment from my presence, my blubbering like a fool in public, or for some other reason, I wasn't sure, they ushered Jim and me away from the crowd and into a private room of a nearby house. There we sat for a long time. I felt numb. Finally, they placed a bowl of rice and sauce in front of us to eat. We ate in silence, not sure what would happen next. This was uncharted territory. Everything was confusing. I had no choice but to wait, trust, and pray everything would be okay. After a while, they ushered us out, and we returned home.

Afterward, we spent several hours going with the police and the governor to the accident scene to record the details of what happened. They were unexpectedly gracious and consoling. I knew it could have been so much worse. I was thankful that my colleague Stevanie, trained in crisis response, came up on Sunday and Monday to help Jim, Andrea, and me begin to debrief and work through the grief. I was also grateful for a missionary family in town who took Andrea and our children in while Jim and I dealt with the situation with the family and the police. I spent a good part of Monday returning to the police station, recounting again to them what happened, filling out reports, and returning to the hospital and pharmacy to pay all the bills. Friends, African and missionary alike, came to visit and brought food.

Tuesday morning was spent going out with the police to the girl's village with a gift for the family. We finalized statements with the family and all of us together as witnesses. Andrea also went along, needing some closure. When we arrived, the faces of the relatives were still somber. Only the older men smiled; the handshakes were weak, telling me they were half-hearted and sad. I was afraid of what the men would decide.

I was also afraid to face the parents. I imagined they were unable to grieve adequately on the day of the funeral because they had to put on a stiff upper lip in front of all their guests. I could hear the mother wailing alone in her house. I couldn't imagine how grieved she must be. We sat with the men while waiting for the chief to show up. Finally, he arrived, and they talked for quite a while. Lots of women came out to greet us, but not the mother. I felt compelled to go in and greet her finally. Andrea went too. We saw the couple's only remaining child, a little girl - she was clinging to a relative and fearful of us. It made me wonder what her family had told her.

Then the women sat us down in a room and asked a young teenage boy where the mother was. He looked in at me and said in the local language in a voice that hinted of disrespect, "Is that the one who killed her?" The older women began scolding him. I felt horrible. I could only guess certain ones felt real disdain for me, which they hid just under the surface. They must all be putting on a good front.

Then someone said the mother had gone to the hospital, that she was sick. I was about to leave when the mother came in; she was there all along. She came in with a flat face and a weak handshake, going through the motions. I wished I had not come. I felt terrible and imagined my presence only made her pain worse. I asked her if she was sick, and she told me she ached all over and was hot during the night. I didn't know what to do. She walked out, so I went back out with the men.

Then she and some other women came out and sat there, listening to the men. I sat beside her, feeling awkward. I asked her if she needed a ride to the hospital since she was sick. She refused my help, saying she would go on her own. I felt like my presence was causing her so much pain. It was unbearable. I knew she needed space to grieve through all of this.

We brought a sack of rice and some money, hoping it would contribute to the burden of having to feed all the guests at the funeral. We also presented them with a traditional gift of cola nuts, which we were told was appropriate for such an occasion. The elders presented our gifts to the family, explaining that it was a gesture to show them our sincerity and compassion in some way.

However, they refused the money and the rice, only accepting the cola nuts in honor of the tradition and respect it represented. They said they couldn't take the money and rice, as if they were payment for a life that could not be bought. Then I felt horrible. Did we do the right thing? They said their elders many generations ago always upheld the tradition that only cola would be passed when a bride price was paid or a wrong was done. But money represented a bribe, and they felt that was dishonorable. "Eating the rice would be like eating the child," they said. They couldn't do that.

As the men of the village convened, one of the elders we knew well from the sister village spoke up and bore witness to the help we had given them several years ago. He told them how his village considered us as part of their family. Clearly, God had worked behind the scenes years ago to make this situation a bit more bearable. After more deliberation, the child's village elders declared openly that we were forgiven, and no charges would be pressed. They announced it was "the will of God" and "there was no ill intent." We were relieved, but our hearts were still heavy. The men permitted Jim to respond with a few words. Jim told them we were thankful for their forgiveness but that we would forever be saddened by this tragedy.

It was a difficult day for everyone. It brought all the emotions from the day of the accident back. The family requested we keep our distance for a while since it brought back the memory of the loss to the parents. Now that the formalities were over, we were relieved and thankful that the police had been so kind. No one had caused us the trouble that we had feared. We were also grateful for the family's demonstration of forgiveness.

During the days that followed, I had trouble dealing with the roller coaster of emotions that came in the aftermath of the accident. I was pretty messed up and basically non-functional most of the week. I was confused, discouraged, and just plain exhausted. I felt myself getting irritable at little things, overwhelmed at merely fixing lunch and taking care of everyone else. Every day was a chore. Other people had to cook for me and clean my house. Grief overwhelmed me, and I couldn't sleep. Finally, someone went to the pharmacy and got me a sedative to help me sleep.

When Stevanie came to minister to us, I told her I felt alone and that God had abandoned me. She told me I could trust that God never left me and that he was going through this with me. But I didn't feel it and didn't believe it. My mind kept telling me that my life as I knew it was over.

I struggled to pray; I couldn't get myself to even open my Bible. I felt bitter and numb. Like Job, who, after he had lost everything, tore his robes and fell to the ground in worship,[2] I tried to find comfort in singing worship songs, as I had so many times before, but it was tough. I tried to listen to the words and believe them. I tried to trust God, even though I couldn't imagine what he was doing in this situation. I knew that, despite my limited understanding, God was sovereign. I had no choice but to place my life in his hands and trust in his strength to keep pressing forward even though darkness was closing in around me.

Andrea had brought with her a newly released CD from Casting Crowns and had given it to us as a gift. The lyrics of one song echoed the cries of my heart:

I was sure by now that you would have reached down,
And wiped our tears away, stepped in and saved the day,
But once again, I say "Amen," and it's still raining.
As the thunder rolls, I barely hear
you whisper through the rain, "I'm with you."
And as your mercy falls,
I raise my hands and praise the God who gives,
and takes away
I'll praise you in this storm, and I will lift my hands
For you are who you are, no matter where I am
Every tear I've cried, you hold in your hand
You never left my side, and though my heart is torn
I will praise you in this storm.
I remember when I stumbled in the wind,
You heard my cry, you raised me up again,
My strength is almost gone;
how can I carry on if I can't find you
I lift my eyes unto the hills;
where does my help come from?
My help comes from the Lord,
the Maker of Heaven and Earth.[3]

During the weeks that followed, little things triggered anxiety and panic attacks. I became fearful that people who knew about the accident might try to retaliate. It was hard to trust God when all my mind wanted to do was fret and worry. I tried to busy myself with housework and do the next thing, but it was nearly impossible to get the events of the accident out of my mind.

Over the next month, I continued to struggle with guilt about the accident. I questioned why God would let this happen to me. The "what ifs" began to pile up again in my mind. I kept asking myself what would have happened if I had not gone on the outing that day. What if I had listened to my inner voice telling me I should have canceled the trip? What if I had done this or that instead and delayed my passage by that particular place by a few minutes or even seconds? I kept retracing my steps, wondering where I had made a wrong turn, where I had perhaps missed out on the Holy Spirit's whisper to take a different path. I wondered if there was some hidden sin in my life that I had not addressed. Was God punishing me? Logic told me that God didn't always work that way, but my emotions kept getting the best of me.

There was another nagging question in my mind: Why didn't God show up and answer my prayer when I needed him the most? I laid hands over the girl many times and prayed over her in the emergency room, believing with all my heart that God could and would heal her! Never in my life had I prayed with such confidence! My faith was greater than a mustard seed that day! I prayed for those mountains to move, and I believed! Yet she died anyway. Was God done listening to my prayers? Was I not praying hard enough? Was I arrogant to assume my prayers could do anything?

One evening a plumber we had hired to do a job told us he knew the girl, was from the village, and was related to her. When I learned this, I got hot, flushed, and concerned. My mind became paranoid with the fear of retaliation. I feared for my children. A few days later, a man and woman who had previously been in one of Jim's literacy classes and part of his village Scripture-checking group had heard about the incident from their neighbors. While Jim and I were working in the office, they came to our house to offer us a small amount of money as a "funeral gift."

I told them I was not worthy of it. But they just kept reaffirming me. I burst into tears. I continued to weep for a long time after they left. I felt some release that day, but Jim was more subdued than his usual jovial self.

In the weeks following the accident, I looked back at all the emails we had written to prayer warriors over the past years, and I began to see a clear pattern. Each time we sent out a victory letter, something bad happened afterward. One night at the weekly prayer meeting with the missionaries in our town, we began talking about the traumas and unfortunate events in the past two years that had happened to missionaries who worked among the same people as we did. Our family had had two medical evacuations, then our near miss in Chicago. Other missionaries had multiple medical evacuations, and another was in a terrible car accident. One woman lost the use of her leg due to mysterious knee pain, and another missionary couple barely escaped their crashed plane before it exploded. Others were caught up in a huge legal dispute with one of their workers. Multiple families experienced unexplained illnesses that were only healed with prayer and the laying on of hands. One missionary even reported hearing of leaders of this ethnic group in one region who had come together and put a curse on the missionaries, which would force them all to leave. Seeing this pattern gave me a new perspective.

Here we were, in the final weeks of the read-through of our New Testament translation. A work that had begun decades earlier by colleagues was now finally coming to fruition. Could this be yet another attack of Satan to thwart God's plan and discourage us?

Jim had also grown greatly discouraged and angry since the accident. Jim struggled to see God's purpose in it all and was losing sleep over it. One night he finally prayed that if these thoughts were from Satan, God would take them from him and give him a restful night's sleep. To his relief, he slept well all night and woke up refreshed, the thoughts gone from his mind. We all became keenly aware that something was happening in the spiritual realm that we did not see. The enemy was real. We knew he would love nothing more than to bring us down.

As we all sat together that night in the prayer meeting, recounting the details of Satan's attacks and discouragement, we reflected on how God was working in each situation. As I looked back on the events of those weeks following the accident, I could see many ways how God, in his gentle kindness, did show up. The village and the police were kind and did not consider the accident my fault. It could have been so much worse. The African friends who worked with Jim reassured me. Colleagues came to help us debrief. Dear friends came over on many occasions to cheer me up. Many came alongside me and prayed with me and for me. Even a drunk man showed up at the accident scene to reassure me that everything would be okay.

Tears came to my eyes as I considered God's care for me, and I realized he was indeed walking through this with me. I became mindful of how Satan, in all his craftiness, could skillfully weave lies that blind us from the truth. In my mind, I had believed the lies, and they were preventing me from seeing the truth.

Our adoption process also weighed heavily on my mind. We were in the middle of it, already having filled out mountains of paperwork. We had obtained a clean police report and FBI clearance for the international adoption of two children. Although I was not guilty of any crime, I now had a police record in our host country because of the accident. I prayed that no one would find out or hold that against us in the adoption process.

Chapter Seventeen

THE AFTERMATH

"We are hard pressed on every side, but not crushed; perplexed, but not in despair; persecuted, but not abandoned; struck down, but not destroyed." (2 Corinthians 4:8-9, NIV)

About a month after the accident, things seemed to calm down a bit. We were trying to get back to a sense of normalcy. Then one day, we received a summons to appear before the local judge. Worried, we packed ourselves up, along with one of our trusted African co-workers, and headed to the judge's office. The judge explained that I should remain at home and not travel anywhere until they could hold a hearing and review the case. This meant I was being put on a form of house arrest.

When we asked for clarification, he made it clear that there would be a government trial, apart from the girl's family, to determine if I had done anything in the accident that constituted a crime and warranted consequences. When we asked for an explanation of the "consequences," he hummed and hawed a bit before mentioning, "All of this could, of course, be taken care of by paying a large fine." Finally, it all became clear: we were being extorted for a bribe.

Even if we felt that what he was doing was corrupt, we were the foreigners in this situation, completely at his mercy. And he knew it. I felt trapped, angry, frustrated, and anxious. I left that day upset all over again; all the emotions of the accident rekindled – salt rubbed into a wound. We knew our organization's position was never to offer bribes. We contacted our mission administrator and arranged for a lawyer to get involved.

For the next month, we waited. We waited for news from the judge's office. My mind went to all the possibilities. What if I ended up in prison after all, due to some corrupt government official's stubborn desire for a bribe? What if I was separated from my family? What if we were no longer able to go through with the adoption? Fear of the what-ifs consumed my thoughts. I couldn't go anywhere.

Now, after all this time, growing to love my African home, growing to love the people, and finally finding my niche in ministry and in my community, I suddenly had a strong sense of dread at being here and a desire to run as far away from this place as possible. I wanted to leave West Africa and never come back. Everything about this place would now constantly remind me of my trauma, fear, and pain. Things could turn for the worse at any moment, and I would be trapped. Like a traumatized war veteran from the 1960s, I wanted to leave this place that had now become my Vietnam.

Once again, we were reeling, feeling in limbo, unable to focus well on our work. But we also spent much time praying over the situation, inviting others to join us. Although I continued to struggle with the feeling that God had abandoned me, I still clung to him. I knew God was God. He was sovereign, and he was my only hope in this world. I tried to flood my mind with more worship music and God's Word, clinging to every verse with hope. I tried to find rest in him from my fears and anxiety; I tried to surrender to his will and rid myself of bitterness. I tried to trust God, even though I didn't understand what he was doing. Even when I didn't feel it.

I prayed to God that he would bring justice to the situation, to make a way for the children we were adopting to finally join our family, and to restore my joy as I read the Psalms:

"*Weeping may stay for the night, but rejoicing comes in the morning.*"[1]

"*I will give thanks to you, LORD, with all my heart; I will tell of all your wonderful deeds. I will be glad and rejoice in you; I will sing the praises of your name, O Most High. My enemies turn back; they stumble and perish before you. For you have upheld my right and my cause, sitting enthroned as the righteous judge. You have rebuked the nations and destroyed the wicked.*"[2]

"*You, LORD, hear the desire of the afflicted; you encourage them, and you listen to their cry, defending the fatherless and the oppressed, so that mere earthly mortals will never again strike terror.*"[3]

My thoughts echoed the words of David as I prayed to God to rescue us from this situation:

"*How long, LORD? Will you forget me forever? How long will you hide your face from me? How long must I wrestle with my thoughts and day after day have sorrow in my heart? ... Look on me and answer, LORD my God. Give light to my eyes, or I will sleep in death. ... But I trust in your unfailing love; my heart rejoices in your salvation. I will sing the LORD's praise, for he has been good to me.*"[4]

By the first of March, unrest broke out again in our host country. People on the streets threatened to overthrow the government if their demands weren't met. All the shops in the market closed, and we could not buy anything. Amidst this, I was summoned to appear before the judge regarding the pending accident case. We took our newly assigned lawyer along with us. The judge was rude and intimidating, and the meeting seemed to accomplish nothing. I became more worried after we met with him.

After asking the missionary community to pray with us again about this matter, Brenda, a missionary colleague from three hours away, called me on the phone. She asked me who the judge was and grew excited when I told her his name.

"That is great," she said, "Because of my prison ministry, I worked extensively with him when he served as a judge here."

"So you know him pretty well?"

"Oh yes. I know him and his family very well. Let me know when you next meet with him, and I'll join you when you go see him."

So, one day in mid-March, Brenda and I headed down to the tribunal together. When we entered the judge's office, he and Brenda greeted each other like old friends. They inquired about each other's families and laughed about old times. Then something amazing began to unfold before my eyes. With her years of experience and knowledge of the local customs and culture, Brenda began recounting the entire history the two of them had together. She pointed out to the judge how kind and "fair" he had been with all the prisoners she had helped get back on their feet. Brenda said she was delighted to hear that he was the judge on my case, knowing she could count on him to treat me fairly. I sat there just listening and observing. When they were finished talking, the room became awkwardly quiet.

Finally, I broke the silence and asked, "What is the next step? When can my lawyer and I meet with you again?"

At that point, the judge, unwilling to lose face in light of Brenda's flattery of his stellar reputation, turned to me and said in French, "You don't need a lawyer, she is your lawyer, and this case is closed."

Stunned and grateful, I shook his hand. Right before we left, however, my relief was kept in check as the judge reminded me of "how things go" in his country.

"Someday, the judge who replaces me or who serves later might come across the case and re-open it," he announced.

Clearly, God had brought Brenda to our aid at just the right time. He had used her faithful years of service and relationship-building in the region to redeem this situation. I was so thankful for God's provision. Finally, we could get back to whatever level of normal we could muster.

But from then on, a constant sense of fear and uncertainty nagged my mind just beneath the surface. Could I ever feel safe in this country? I felt as if I was constantly teetering on the edge of depression. Then, I read the Apostle Paul's words to the Philippians:

"Do not be anxious about anything, but in every situation, by prayer and petition, with thanksgiving, present your requests to God. And the peace of God, which transcends all understanding, will guard your hearts and your minds in Christ Jesus." [5]

I prayed that God would give me the peace and rest my soul needed and that my out-of-control anxiety would subside.

A few days later, the young girl's mother stopped by in the evening to see us. She wanted to let me know that there were no hard feelings between us. Soon we would be able to come to her village and visit if we wanted to do so. I was grateful for her kindness and shared again my deepest sorrow for the accident and her daughter's death. I asked her if I could pray with her, and she agreed. I laid hands on her and prayed that God would grant her the gift of another child soon, not that anything could ever replace the child she had lost.

By the end of March, we traveled to the capital for a mini vacation. I was finally free to travel and needed to get away after two extremely stressful months. While there, I got my thyroid hormone levels tested. The tests confirmed that my levels had been slowly dropping since my surgery a year and a half earlier and were now low. This likely made it even harder for me to emerge from my depression slump. We found thyroid medication at a local pharmacy and arranged for a visitor from the US to bring me antidepressant medications. However, once the medicines came, I did not tolerate them well and felt even worse. Clearly, I had to find another solution for treating my depression.

By the end of April, we finished the final read-through of the New Testament translation and were ready to send it off for the peer review stage. Meanwhile, Jim plowed through the revision work on Genesis and Exodus. I had stopped working on the translation altogether. After the accident, I also stopped seeing patients. Due to stress and a lack of energy, and to give myself time to heal, I continued to keep my duties to a minimum. I needed stability, routine, and an environment as stress-free as possible for my emotional and mental health. The truth was, taking care of patients, especially children, was beginning to trigger my anxiety. I continued schooling Katie and Joshua, cooking, and caring for the house. I spent more time tending to my garden, rekindling my love for art, journaling, and reading my Bible.

Over the summer months, the civil unrest in the country continued to erupt into violence. One day we heard constant gunfire and shouting outside our compound for seven hours straight as the military tried to keep crowds under control. While we stayed safely home, many were wounded and killed that day. Other cases of violence erupted all over the country with similar results. There seemed to be no end to the unrest. We lived off our reserves for a while because markets were closed again.

Additionally, the adoption process became a huge waiting game. There were several obstacles, and Aisha's case was running into many snags. Since the beginning of the process, the US embassy had somehow lost our fingerprints three times. We had to make the arduous eight-hour trip back down to the capital each time to get them redone. It was hard not to grow anxious the longer we waited.

Health-wise, I suffered from intermittent ringing in my right ear that began in March and persisted. Some days it was downright debilitating, causing the room to spin and putting me in bed for most of the day. Sometimes I felt my spirit was unwilling to continue the battle to serve in the ministry we felt called to do. I prayed as David did in Psalm 51 that God would *"grant me a willing spirit to sustain me."* [6]

One day I read where the Apostle Paul encouraged the believers facing trials in 1st century Thessalonica that *"no one would be unsettled by these trials"* and that *"we are destined for them."* [7] I felt like life was an endless string of trials, even more so in our line of work. I remembered when I was young how my culture taught me quite the opposite: we all deserve happiness, safety, peace, and prosperity as expectations rather than the exception. Yet the Scriptures said we were destined for trials. We are told to be encouraged and not to let them unsettle us. My life had already been riddled with overwhelming challenges, yet blessings as well. I was slowly coming to terms with the reality of the human experience on a deeper level. Trials are inevitable for everyone, although some will face more than others. True happiness is not a promise but a choice. I knew that my only real hope was to cling to the hope of heaven.

By October, we had the New Testament and several Old Testament books ready to print. Then we got word that Gabriel's adoption was complete, and he was ready to join our family. We purchased tickets to return to the US for our home assignment so we could proceed to Guatemala to get Gabriel. We were burned out, tired, and needed a break from life in Africa. This had been one of the best and worst terms yet. We had mixed emotions.

As we arrived on the coast, ready to fly out, our PBT team gathered with us and celebrated the completion of the New Testament. It was a bittersweet moment: so much to be thankful for, yet so much sacrifice and hardship to get to this point. My thoughts went to the famous words of the 3rd-century African church father, Tertullian: "*The blood of the martyrs is the seed of the church.*" [8] Though our suffering could not compare to those who lost their lives for their faith throughout church history, it was a sobering thought that our own suffering, sweat, and tears were a part of that history in the making.

A few nights before our flight, we, along with several other American families, were invited to the home of an embassy family for a movie night. Our children had a great time hanging out with the other kids, and we all enjoyed great fellowship. However, as we were leaving, Joshua ran out the front door ahead of us. Not realizing it had just rained and the tile was wet, he slid across the tile porch and fell about four feet to the ground. My gut instinct was to run out after him. Unfortunately, I also slipped, fell, and slid down six steps, hitting my head and back on each step as I went. Joshua turned out to be fine. But I, on the other hand, lay stunned at the bottom of the stairs, barely able to move. Several friends and colleagues rushed out to help me, stabilized my head, and brought me back inside.

It was late at night on the weekend. No hospital would be open, much less equipped to handle a head and back injury. I became nauseous and dizzy. I recognized I was having symptoms of a concussion and was also in a lot of pain. The embassy family graciously let me stay in their home until morning. Jim stayed close by me the whole night, checking on me frequently. The family helped settle our kids in. I dry heaved throughout the night but thankfully felt somewhat better the next morning. However, my back was badly bruised and still very painful as we boarded the plane a few days later for the US.

Chapter Eighteen

STRANGE YET FAMILIAR

A week after returning to the US, Jim and I sat in the Houston airport during a hurricane, making arrangements to find a different flight to Guatemala. The weather delays and flight cancellations caused us to miss our flight. It just seemed like things couldn't be easy for us. We finally arrived in Guatemala City late at night, and a missionary family met us at the airport and took us to their home. We had arranged to stay in their place while they went on home assignment. We were thankful to find a warm bed waiting.

The next morning, we awoke in a strange new country. I felt disoriented and out of sync, as if I was still in Africa, yet in a different dimension. Things were vaguely familiar, yet vastly different. I had been studying Spanish on my own for the past 18 months. But plunging into the Latin American world with few options to speak any English was a whole new level of culture shock. The house worker where we stayed spoke only Spanish. The taxi driver spoke only Spanish. While riding in the taxi, we passed a group of police gathered around a body in the middle of the road. Armed guards were posted at every restaurant and pharmacy. What were we getting ourselves into?

Later that day, the two gals who worked for the adoption agency (and thankfully spoke good English) took us by taxi to the orphanage. Our soon-to-be son, Gabriel, now nearly two years old, had lived there since birth. As we approached, I suddenly got nervous. Would Gabriel like us? How would he react to us?

We first saw Gabriel in the playground. He stared up at us with no expression on his face. I reached down to pick him up, and he seemed comfortable enough. Suddenly a flood of other children approached us and tried to get hugs from us. There were so many needy children wanting attention. I was overwhelmed with emotion and grateful to have the chance to make a difference in at least this one child's life. Soon Gabriel laid his head on my shoulder and fell asleep. Jim and I sat waiting for about an hour while he slept. Then it was lunchtime, and all the children were fed.

I dressed Gabriel in some new clothes and held him for a long time. We talked to him, but he just stared blankly at us. Finally, I got out a couple of books I had brought and some puzzles and toys. He took to the puzzles and books quickly. Soon we had him smiling and laughing. Keeping the other children from coming over and upstaging the event was difficult. But I couldn't refuse them. I had no idea if they would ever have parents. It broke my heart. We played with him for about an hour and then had to leave. We told the matron caring for him that we would return tomorrow to take him with us. Tears welled up in her eyes. She had been through this many times before, but I was sure it was never easy to say goodbye to yet another child.

The next day we took a taxi to Aisha's orphanage. They had told her we were coming, and she was excited to see us. Other children gathered around, watching curiously. She came up to both of us and embraced us. Then the orphanage workers ushered us into a private room where we could get to know her better. She was all hugs and was over-the-top excited. She immediately began calling us "mama" and "papa." She liked the gifts we brought her. She was very intrigued by Jim's beard. She introduced us to all her friends and constantly chattered in Spanish.

When we were ready to leave, they decided it would be fine for Aisha to come and stay with us for a few days in a "foster" arrangement, even though her adoption wasn't even close to being finalized. They packed her a bag of things, and she couldn't wait for the "carro" to come.

Later that evening, our adoption facilitator, Sonja, brought Gabriel by. They had signed off his adoption, and he was ours now. He cried when he left the orphanage and was in a daze when they brought him to us. It was late in the evening. He went right to sleep in our bed. Aisha also wanted to sleep in our room, saying she was "miedo," scared. Gabriel had a cough and an obvious ear infection. Our hosts' dog whimpered outside the window all night. Needless to say, we all had a restless night.

The first week with our two toddlers proved to be challenging at times. We found ourselves navigating occasional temper tantrums, which were sometimes dramatic and drawn out. We wondered how we would be able to respond to the unique needs of these children, who already had a rocky start to their young lives. With this new stress, little sleep, and a sore back from the incident a week earlier, I had my own little meltdown and a few panic attacks. I had moments when I wondered why I was there and what on earth I was doing. At other times, though, I took a deep breath and watched as the kids grew to trust us more. They played together well, laughed and giggled, fell asleep in our arms, and settled into a routine. Overall, Aisha and Gabriel seemed like good kids but craved love, attention, and stability. I prayed that God would give us wisdom and help us give them the love they needed.

After a week in Guatemala, Jim returned to the US to be with Katie and Joshua, whom we had left with my mom in St. Louis. I remained in Guatemala for the rest of the month, awaiting word from the embassy about Gabriel's US visa. I returned Aisha to her orphanage and tried to adjust to living alone with a two-year-old in a foreign country. My days were filled with trying to navigate the neighborhood markets, banks, pharmacies, and doctor appointments for Gabriel, all while attempting to use my broken Spanish.

It was a trying month. I realized how much I depended on Jim for emotional support. Even though we sent emails every day, it wasn't the same as being together. At times I didn't feel safe. In the evenings, I sometimes heard gunfire or fireworks. I was never sure which. This rattled my nerves and triggered me. I didn't know how to interpret these familiar sounds in an unfamiliar place where I didn't know the rules or what was normal. All I could do was pray for God's protection.

Around the end of the month, I anxiously awaited my appointment with the US embassy to get Gabriel's visa and take him home to join our family. When the day of the appointment arrived, I sat down with Gabriel in the waiting area of the embassy, along with about 45 other American families, each with their adopted children in tow. I waited as they called each name out, one by one. At the end of the long day, Gabriel and I were the last ones waiting. No one called our names. Finally, I walked up to the window and asked the lady there if they would still call on us. She asked me my name and the name of the child I was adopting. After I told her, she informed me that his visa was not there.

I felt a sense of dread and panic rush through my head. Distraught, I asked her what the next step would be. I told her that our flight left Wednesday afternoon. She told me I would have to come back Wednesday morning before my flight to see if things were ready.

I left the embassy reeling. My mind began going over the past year. This was a year I did not want to live through again. First, the accident, then my thyroid, my ear problem, the civil unrest, the fall on the stairs, the traveling, culture shock in Guatemala, being alone without Jim, the challenges with the adoption, and the challenges with our new children. Now, this.

The thought of returning to the US without Gabriel, now that he had bonded with me over the past month, was more than I could bear. How would he handle abandonment? The stress was just too much. I knew trials were supposed to make you stronger, but I felt like I was getting weaker and weaker and not coping well at all. Once again, I wanted to crawl into a hole and make it all disappear.

Wednesday morning, November 9th, came. My bags packed, Gabriel in my arms, I headed off to the embassy early. After waiting anxiously, they called me to the window. Apparently, there was a problem. It was the fingerprints, once again. Unfortunately, our fingerprint report had never come. I argued with the lady, pointing out that we could not possibly have gotten this far without the fingerprints. Nevertheless, she said they never received the actual report. Finally, desperate, I asked her if we could get them done again here. She shook her head no. Her answer was not what I wanted to hear.

"What should we do now?" I asked.

"You will have to return to the US and get it all straightened out," she replied.

"Without Gabriel?"

"Yes," she answered. "He cannot get on the plane without a visa."

I left the embassy devastated. I found a park bench outside, sat Gabriel down, and broke into tears. I was beside myself. Just then, Gabriel decided to fill his diaper with an unpleasant load and began crying loudly. I had to change him out in the open. I cried even harder.

Two security guards came over to see if I was okay. All I could do was blubber in broken Spanish, trying to explain to them through the tears what was going on. I'm sure I was an embarrassment. I was barely holding myself together.

Then I thought of Sonja. Maybe she would know what to do. So, I called her on the cell phone she gave me when I arrived. She graciously offered to come by, pick me up, and take me to the airport. She said we would figure the rest out.

I was incredibly relieved when Sonja arrived. She was like an angel in disguise. As we traveled to the airport, I explained my dilemma. Sonja decided she could take Gabriel to the orphanage where he had been living and see if they would temporarily take him back until all of this could get sorted out. If not, she said she and her mother would personally care for him until we returned to get him. I was overwhelmed with gratitude. Sonja's heart was so big and generous. It was clear she loved these children as much as I did.

We finally arrived at the airport and stopped at the departure gate. Everything was happening so fast. I couldn't believe I was leaving without Gabriel. I had envisioned this moment for so long. Now everything seemed hopeless. As I handed Gabriel to Sonja, he began whimpering, reaching his arms out to me. Tears formed in my eyes as I kissed him and said goodbye. His whimpering turned to loud screaming as I walked away.

My heart was broken. It was all I could do to fight back the tears as I boarded the plane. With Gabriel's visa in limbo and Aisha's adoption process at a standstill, I had no idea how long it would be before I would see either of the children again, if ever. I prayed that somehow we would figure everything out and that this separation would not cause undue trauma for these two precious children. It was already having an impact on me.

I reunited with the family back in St. Louis. After a good night's rest, Jim and I headed to the government building downtown to figure out what could be done. We felt like the craziest rollercoaster ride was almost over, but we were now bracing ourselves again, hanging on tight for yet another wild ride. After quite a few hassles, we found a helpful employee who seemed to know what to do. The bottom line was that we had to get the fingerprints done yet again. Then we had to file all the paperwork over again. But of course, for an extra $200 fee, they would expedite everything.

We willingly did what we were told. At this point, we just wanted it all behind us. Within a few days, we had another appointment at the Embassy in Guatemala to pick up a visa for Gabriel. This time I called ahead and asked to speak to the same lady who had turned me down before. I asked her for assurance that this time all the proper paperwork was in hand before we flew down again. She reassured me that everything was a "go." This time Jim planned to go, as I wasn't sure I had the emotional fortitude to go through a repeat experience. So, on November 19th, Jim boarded another plane for Guatemala.

Thankfully, this time around, everything went smoothly. Sonja brought Gabriel to Jim. Jim got our son's visa and boarded the plane back to the US with Gabriel two days later. In the very early hours of Thanksgiving Day morning, 2006, our family stood at the arrival gate at the St. Louis airport to welcome back Jim and a sleepy Gabriel in his arms. It was a sweet reunion. We headed straight to an extended family gathering where aunts, uncles, and cousins met Gabriel for the first time. We had a wonderful day of celebration and thankfulness in more ways than one.

We were grateful Gabriel was finally home with us. Still, we worried about Aisha's adoption. It weighed heavily on us that everything seemed to be at an impasse. We knew that the only thing we could do was to relinquish control over the situation, which we never had in the first place, and place it all in God's hands. Emotionally, we had to let go and operate under the assumption that her adoption might never happen. When we did that, our hearts finally began to find rest.

Reflecting on all that we had been through, the words of Psalm 91:4 came to mind:

"He will cover you with his feathers. He will shelter you with his wings. His faithful promises are your armor and protection."[1]

What a year it had been. We had finalized the New Testament and
Genesis, endured many traumas, crises, medical issues, and other
challenges, and packed up our home. We had been in dozens of airplanes,
cars, and taxis, traveled thousands of miles through five countries,
welcomed an orphan into our family, and made many other transitions.

I thought back to my training years earlier when new recruits for
our organization underwent psychological evaluations. One of the tests
measured the stressful events and transitions you experienced and gave
you a score indicating the likelihood of danger to your health. I imagined
our score was way off the charts. Needless to say, we were weary. But
I knew that God had carried us and sustained us through everything.
Now, back in the US, with the holidays approaching, we looked forward
to a period of rest.

Chapter Nineteen

RUMORS OF WAR

The civil unrest in our West African host country had worsened while we were in the US preparing for Gabriel's arrival home. The day before Thanksgiving Day, while we anxiously awaited Jim's return to the US with Gabriel, we received some hard news from one of our West Africa team leaders. One of our fellow missionary families was held at gunpoint at their home, robbed, and left injured. Moreover, our vehicle, which our colleagues had been driving at the time, was stolen in the attack. We were greatly discouraged. Our colleagues had been traumatized. And the prospect of raising another $50,000 for a new vehicle seemed daunting.

However, we quickly enlisted a whole host of prayer warriors to pray for our colleagues' healing and recovery and for the missing vehicle to be returned. Miraculously, one week later, the local police found our car abandoned and unharmed, with the keys and all the papers still in place. Relieved, we tried to find time to enjoy the holidays with family in St. Louis.

Meanwhile, Jim collaborated with a colleague to print our translation of Genesis and ship it to West Africa. Additionally, he finished the type-setting and layout of the entire New Testament. Unfortunately, there were multiple setbacks. First, Jim's computer crashed in the process. Then, another colleague helping with type-setting and other tasks had four computers crash.

Now back in the US, I finally saw a specialist who diagnosed my ongoing ringing ear problem and dizziness as Meniere's disease. He tried several medications that were sometimes helpful but didn't take the symptoms away completely. The specialist said I would have to radically reduce my salt intake. Although this did bring some relief, it was an adjustment.

By mid-January, the crisis in our West African host country had reached a fever pitch. Inflation skyrocketed, and food became unaffordable for the average person. Water and electricity were scarce. Markets, schools, taxi stations, hospitals, shops, government offices, and public services all closed. Masses of people began to protest. Workers went on strike. Violent protests broke out, resulting in many deaths. Our colleagues holed up in their homes for days, which turned into weeks.

The situation continued to deteriorate over the next month. Conditions became so extremely hazardous that our colleagues and most other expatriates made the decision to evacuate. Some were able to board either commercial or military flights. Others took long journeys through rugged bush terrain, guided by GPS and word of mouth, across the borders to neighboring countries. My brother and his family were among them. Families were sometimes separated for weeks.

Despite all the challenges, many of our colleagues reported being warmly welcomed in villages and assisted by many gracious people along the way. Eventually, everyone on our team, including my brother and his family, safely returned to Dallas for debriefing. I was thankful we were already safely on the other side of the Atlantic. I was sure I would not have handled the added trauma of the evacuation in my fragile emotional state. We traveled to Dallas to join our team.

During the debriefing, I met with a counselor and formally discussed some of my traumas for the first time. My counselor said that danger was a random, rare occurrence for most people and that our fears were often unfounded. I could see his point for most people, but that certainly didn't apply to those of us serving in West Africa. I asked him if a soldier in battle, for example, could really expect never to get shot at. I recognized that God had repeatedly delivered me and many of my colleagues from danger. However, I couldn't get past the fact that danger was just simply more common, and safety was an illusion in the part of the world where we worked. My fears and the fears of others had come true too many times.

Eventually, the counselor admitted that danger was more of a threat where we served overseas, and our colleagues and we had faced "more than our fair share" of crises. But what was I going to do with that information? I didn't want to accept it. I still struggled with the reality that living in West Africa presented a genuine threat to our safety. Yet my faith demanded that I sacrifice my own needs and safety to serve and reach the lost. I faced a dilemma. The years of stress and crisis had eaten away my confidence, resilience, and even my faith at times. I wasn't okay with that. The words of David in Psalm 23 had once been a comfort to me:

"Even though I walk through the darkest valley, I will fear no evil,..." [1]

Now these were hard words for me to swallow. The fact was, when I was honest with myself, I *did* fear evil.

As we met together, our larger West African team discussed possible strategies for when and if we could return to West Africa and how that might look. Jim and I began formulating our own contingency plan in the event we could not return. One of the options was to remain in the US and work remotely. This process came as a relief in many ways. We could envision continuing the work we were passionate about while staying a safe distance from the danger.

Still, there was a nagging conflict inside me. There were parts of West Africa that I missed: my home, my friends, the warm climate, and the laid-back culture and lifestyle to which I had grown accustomed. I missed ministry victories, morning walks greeting the neighbors, quiet afternoons sitting with the local ladies under the trees having warm conversations, and the many memories we had made while raising our children there. Part of Africa had merged with my soul and could never be separated. Yet the harsh realities, traumas, and fear hung over me like a black cloud, and I couldn't shake it.

For the time being, we focused our attention on bringing Aisha home. Then, in early March, we received the surprising news that her adoption paperwork was completed. We could only view this as a miraculous turn of events. We could bring our new daughter home by the end of the month. During the last week of March 2007, I traveled to Guatemala alone, armed with a suitcase full of new clothes, toys, and gifts, ready to woo our little girl into our lives. I was fearful that she would not want to come with me. Thankfully, she was cheerful and cooperative. On the plane ride home, I rested easy as I listened to her sing aloud in Spanish so everyone could hear, "I'm going to America! I'm going to Grandma's house! I have a family!" This time, traveling back to the US from Guatemala, I shed tears of joy.

Once back in St. Louis, our family was reunited. What a joy it was to watch all four children giggling together, chasing one another through the house, and finally being a family together. There were challenges ahead, to be sure. But I soaked in every bit of that moment while it lasted.

In the following months, we discovered that Aisha's paperwork was not all in order. She had not been granted citizenship, so we would have to undergo a re-adoption process through the US court system. We weren't sure how long it would take. But with things in West Africa "on hold" for the moment, we knew we could take all the time we needed.

Besides, nothing seemed as daunting as what we had already experienced. The fact that our toddlers were home helped put us at ease. For the moment, we celebrated our children's arrival. We also celebrated Jim's completion of his master's degree and received printed copies of the translations of the New Testament and the book of Genesis we had completed that year.

Our summer was filled with traveling, speaking at churches, and visiting friends and family all over the US. We were refreshed in many ways. Over time, we felt we should return to West Africa if the doors reopened. But I had mixed feelings. I knew returning was the "right" thing to do, as far as our duty and obligations were concerned. But for the first time, I did not have the enthusiasm and eagerness to return as I had before. I think more than anything, I wanted to prove to myself that I could do it, that I could face my fears, and that the traumas would no longer paralyze me.

I prayed that God would restore my passion and sense of purpose in serving in West Africa. Most of all, I prayed that God would help me overcome my fear. I knew that, for myself, this time, a return to Africa would be more out of a sense of obligation and duty rather than desire.

In the meantime, we began looking at houses in the event that we could not return to West Africa. After exploring all the options, we decided to purchase a piece of land with the money Jim had saved up from his Navy pension. We felt that we could eventually build on it should the need arise.

By mid-July, Aisha's citizenship was granted. By August, the re-adoption process was completed. The unrest had calmed down, and things began to look favorable for a return to West Africa. But one more thing stood in the way. Because of my ongoing health issues, my doctor determined I needed a hysterectomy. We knew now that having more children biologically was out of the question. I had to let go of that dream. I required a two-month recovery time afterward. With this in mind, we set our departure for October. After a painful recovery from surgery, we had an uneventful return to our home in West Africa. This would be my fifth term.

Chapter Twenty

A SOBERING TRUTH

Back in our African home, we once again began "digging out" the dirt and mildew from our year away – cleaning and setting things up for another term. Katie and Joshua enjoyed showing Aisha and Gabriel the ropes of living there. The kids explored all the old toys, which were new to the little ones, and arranged things to make room for two more. We soon settled into a routine: I schooled the kids and treated patients while Jim worked on the translation. He and our co-translator had rough-drafted the entire Old Testament in previous years. Now Jim needed to get down to the nitty-gritty of comprehension-checking the translation in the village setting, starting with the book of Exodus. I had to take it easy, as my back was still bothering me, and I was still only two months out of surgery.

We dealt with the same daily challenges of malfunctioning equipment, non-stop neighbors and their children coming to our home for medical treatment, and constant interruptions. Only this time, we had four kids to raise and educate instead of two. As before, we had to be ready at all times of the day to receive guests, whether African neighbors or missionaries passing through, and show hospitality. Sometimes the interruptions were welcome; at other times, they took an emotional toll on us. We grew tired more easily and felt we were less resilient.

Overall, I felt more subdued than my usual self: not really depressed as much as sad. I didn't feel as joyful as I had hoped I would be. Something had definitely changed. I had joy in the Lord but longed more than ever for heaven. I prayed for God to continue giving me strength so that someday I would thrive once again rather than merely survive.

Despite my sadness, we continued to see God's Word bear fruit in our community. Our colleagues were distributing copies of Scripture portions we had printed, and people were hungry for more. Scripture portions were being sold in the markets in surrounding regions. We continued to hear testimonies of lives changed and saved by reading God's Word in their own language. This was an encouragement. Our labor had not been in vain.

Then one day, some neighbors brought me a child who had been sick for three months. He was lethargic, severely jaundiced, and almost comatose. The family had already exhausted all other options. Their son had received blood transfusions and multiple treatments at other hospitals. Now the family told me I was their only hope. I wasn't sure what was wrong with him. So, I treated him for malaria, not sure it would help.

The next day, they brought him back to me. He was in a bad state, as yellow as ever, hallucinating and biting his mother. I wondered if he was suffering from hepatic encephalopathy, a condition associated with liver failure in which toxic ammonia levels build up, causing confusion and hallucinations. She began begging me to help her, insisting that I was holding back some treatment that could help him. I knew there might be hope in the US or other more developed countries, but here in West Africa, nothing short of a miracle could save him. I felt helpless. I assured her that I had nothing else. I tried to explain to the family that if the other hospitals couldn't help the child and my medicine didn't work, all we could do was pray. Jim came outside, and together we laid hands on the young boy and prayed for him.

The next morning, word arrived that the sick boy had been taken to the local hospital, where they confirmed that nothing more could be done to help him. It was only a matter of time before he would die. So, the family took him home. About an hour later, a messenger informed us that he had passed away.

Without warning, the news triggered a sudden, debilitating spiral of autonomic responses in my body. My emotions began spinning out of control. My heart raced. My breathing became shallow, and my chest became tight. My head was pounding. Panic, fear, and depression filled my mind. Post-traumatic stress was rushing back with full force. The announcement that another child died, and this one in my care, instantly took me back to my dark place and the emotions I experienced after the accident, now almost two years prior. I tried to control my breathing to calm myself down so I could think. Even my best efforts were not very successful.

For the next several days, I stewed over the implications of what had happened. Once again, we had laid hands on a sick child and prayed over him in Jesus' name to be healed. Why had the Great Physician himself chosen not to heal him? Or the little girl in the accident two years earlier? Or so many others? I felt so helpless and powerless as a Christian, and doubts about my faith crept in again. Maybe my faith wasn't good enough for God. I resented being the one that everyone came to for answers, the one everyone depended on. I had failed them. I felt like I failed God.

I began struggling with being in West Africa all over again. I wanted to run away and never come back. I told Jim I didn't think I had it in me to treat pediatric patients anymore. I did not recognize the lies my depression was telling me. Nor did I see how Satan was using this situation to raise doubts about my faith.

About a week later, Joshua had a close call. His fingers were injured when they were accidentally slammed in a car door. My anxiety skyrocketed. That night I dreamed that Aisha drowned, and I couldn't revive her. I startled awake, breathing heavily, thanking God that it was only a dream. I began fearing for my children's safety and worrying about them constantly. Not a day went by that some mishap occurred involving one of our children getting hurt. Each event triggered waves of emotional reactions from previous trauma held in check just under the surface. Each time I felt my heart and emotions couldn't handle one more crisis.

Life has plenty of challenges for everyone, to be sure. Trying to meet the needs of four or more kids is no easy task. But as the added stress of living cross-culturally returned with full force, not to mention the triggers from my past traumas, I struggled more and more to cope. With each new crisis, my internal conflict with being in Africa returned. I prayed to God to give me the courage to do life in this place.

What's more, the local church had all but fallen apart. There were believers who abandoned their faith, and some of our colleagues left for good. Other Christian workers in our town were discouraged. My disillusionment grew stronger.

Depression set in once again by December and was so strong that I despaired of life. I was convinced that my life meant nothing and there was hardly reason to go on living. Only the knowledge of God's love and grace toward me served as my guardrail.

I cried out to God for Christ's return and that he would remove us from the stresses of this life and end the struggle we had to face in this world. The task God had called us to do was impossible by human standards. I never felt as inadequate as I did at that moment. But I kept those thoughts in check by sheer force of will, knowing from experience that these emotions would pass with time. I also knew my husband and children needed me.

Once again, I knew I could do nothing but lean on the Lord and wait for him to restore a sense of peace in my mind and spirit. I prayed that if I had to continue living in this place, God would restore my desire to do so.

We traveled to the capital for PBT team meetings in the following weeks. The time of fellowship and encouragement from our colleagues was helpful. We also looked forward to a week of retreat up country with several other families.

As we stopped to rest in a wooded area alongside the road, a swarm of some of the most beautiful butterflies we had ever seen descended upon us. It reminded me of the time in Papua New Guinea years earlier when my younger self ran barefoot, fearless, and carefree through the forest chasing butterflies. I had been at one with what I sensed was God's calling in my life, blissfully unaware of the trauma that lay before me. Years later, parked alongside this road in West Africa, these butterflies were a gentle reminder of God's care for me in a darker time and a refreshing diversion, even if only for a moment.

Once we arrived at our destination for the retreat, we enjoyed fellowship with friends. The kids swung on the vines in the forest, chased more butterflies, built bamboo forts, and watched the colobus monkeys play in the trees. We all sat around the campfire in the evening. These precious moments of fellowship and pause were life-giving, even when living out of suitcases quickly lost its appeal.

Once we returned home, we put up our meager Christmas decorations and tried to get into the Christmas spirit. Not soon afterward, all the children came down with horrible coughs. Aisha's fever spiked. She cried at night, complaining of neck pain, saying she couldn't move her legs. At first, I feared viral meningitis. Unsure of what to do, I treated her for malaria on a hunch. The next day she began feeling better. But she continued to remain tired and clingy all week. Still, I was so grateful that the outcome was not as I had feared. I felt myself slowly emerging from my dark place.

Celebrating Christmas with our small missionary community seemed to erase all the cares away for a moment. This Christmas was our first "normal" Christmas in Africa in a long time. It was quiet, slow, and uneventful – just what we needed. No crisis. No travel. No emergency evacuations. No living out of suitcases. We were safe. We were home. I found joy in the simple moments, like reading the Christmas story to the children and feeling satisfied knowing I had imparted something of eternal value to my family. We baked cookies, decorated ornaments, sang Christmas carols every evening before bed, and introduced our two newest family members to the sweet traditions our family cherished – traditions we would continue for years to come.

On Christmas morning, I thanked God for a good night's rest, sipping a hot cup of tea on my porch, listening to the peaceful sound of birds singing in the tranquility of the morning, and the smell of savannah grass in the cool, dry morning air of this part of West Africa. It reminded me of our first Christmas here ten years earlier. At the time, it had not been very noteworthy. But now, the memory held a special place in my heart.

The kids woke up, and Jim read the Christmas story to everyone. Then the kids opened all their gifts, gasping with glee and chattering non-stop. They played so well together, spreading trash, new toys, train sets, crafts, and more all over the house. It was a huge mess, but I soaked in every moment. This was home – a place filled with activities, laughter, and joy. I felt blessed and thankful for all God had given us and for a few weeks of peace and rest in a corrupt, dark, and suffering world.

That year the Christmas message gave me real hope as I contemplated the best gift of all, the Savior God sent us in Jesus. God entered our fallen world and intervened powerfully by doing the only thing that could bring real hope. I knew his gift was needed to clean up this messy world, and I knew I needed him to fix my own brokenness as well.

As we moved into the new year, 2008, there were once again rumors of civil unrest. Tensions between civilians and the government began mounting. We prayed that they would not come to a head as they had in the past year. But we were advised to start putting our contingency plans into action once again. We updated our contact information and evacuation lists. We stocked up on supplies, medicines, and fuel, which had already become scarce.

People began retreating to their home villages to avoid any potential conflicts in the towns and cities. It was difficult not to become stressed as threats of unrest and evacuation loomed heavily over us again. We stayed home and remained inconspicuous. We avoided travel and tried to keep our stress levels low as possible. Thankfully, the rumors died down, and nothing came of it. We breathed a sigh of relief.

Chapter Twenty-One

TURNING POINT

T he following months of early 2008 were a flurry of activities. We hosted an intern who went with colleagues on an 80-mile, three-week trek in the 100-degree African heat. They shouldered over 200 Scripture portions and health teaching books to people who had previously been untouched by the Gospel. However, our intern became deathly ill from dehydration and couldn't complete the trek. Then Jim traveled to assist one of our PBT families after their house burned down. Believers and missionaries working among the people group we served came together for a dedication ceremony of the New Testament we had completed. We also celebrated Easter with a large group of believers in a nearby town and witnessed several baptisms.

On one trip upcountry to visit some of our colleagues, we met another missionary couple who had previously worked elsewhere in West Africa experiencing civil war. All the local people in the area had fled during the war, but the missionaries had stayed. When rebel soldiers came to their town, they interrogated the couple, even holding them at gunpoint several times. They eventually had to evacuate, leaving their home and possessions behind for the soldiers to confiscate. Years later, when this family attempted to return, they shipped a new container of personal possessions and supplies to the country. Their container finally arrived at the port, only to be destroyed in a freak explosion.

One would think this might have discouraged them to the point of not wanting to return. But instead, they returned to another region, this time with minimal possessions. They seemed quite content, even very happy. I asked the wife why she was so optimistic. She said that she had learned not to grow attached to things and to live simply instead. There was less to grieve over that way. This liberated them so much that they had learned to be happy in the moment, happy with the blessings that daily came their way, and happy with relationships and whatever divine appointments God in his grace would orchestrate.

From then on, I began to consider how I could adopt that approach and downsize my own possessions. I had become attached to the things I had brought to make my life more pleasant and bearable in this place. These things had given me a false sense of security.

One day, we hired some young men to cut down a tree in our yard that was blocking our solar panels from the sun. Distracted by a branch that was about to fall on and destroy some of our personal items, I laid down my phone and walked away. After the workers left, we looked everywhere for the phone but couldn't find it. Our guard knew the workers, so he went to them and questioned them about the phone. They denied taking it, but one of them confessed the next day.

By the end of the week, we were surprised to learn that three men were arrested and jailed because of the incident. Their families bailed them out and required them to make amends with us. Although we were grateful that the outcome was positive, the ordeal consumed a lot of our time and energy and set off many post-traumatic stress triggers. The multiple trips to the jail and police station, plus sorting out the details with authorities, stirred up emotions from the accident two years prior. My anxiety kept me from sleeping well and being at peace.

A few days later, we traveled to the capital for a meeting with our PBT colleagues from around the country. My stress level was once again very high, and my emotions were raw. I found that I was having memory lapses. People would entrust me with tasks, but I would not remember being asked to do them. I had no recollection of conversations I had had with individuals. Was I losing my mind?

During a devotional time that week, our director shared a message from the book of Joshua. God had commanded the armies of Israel to walk around the city of Jericho many times before the city fell. On the seventh day, the Israelites walked around the city seven times. The people were weary but kept moving because God had commanded them to do so. Only then did the walls fall down. I felt like that's where we were. We were weary, pressing on only because we believed God told us to do so. The journey was getting harder, not easier. We knew that we could only move forward with God's strength.

During the meetings, a licensed trauma counselor had come to meet with anyone who had a need since many of us had been through so much trauma and stress. I had been struggling for so long that I gratefully took him up on his offer. During that counseling session, the counselor shared his own family's story. Since he, too, had been through some unimaginable trauma living in Africa, I realized that I could trust him with my story.

I told him every traumatic incident I could remember over the next couple of hours. He helped me unpack what I had been through over the years, particularly the traumas in Africa. It was the most liberating thing I had ever done. I felt listened to and understood. He affirmed that I wasn't crazy. He told me that with over 24 critical incidents identified and non-stop stress with no opportunity to recover physically, no wonder I was a mess.

On top of that, having only part of my thyroid left, my body could not respond to the stress in the normal way, and this was affecting my memory. He officially diagnosed me with PTSD and explained how my reactions were unsurprising, considering my experiences. I finally felt like the healing process could begin. I wasn't crazy. We arranged to have informal "group therapy" with other colleagues who had been traumatized, which was helpful.

In May, more civil unrest ensued in our part of West Africa. The military in our town walked the streets, firing bullets into the air to show their displeasure with the government. Again, we found ourselves lying low, staying home and out of harm's way. The country's economy was deteriorating, and the cost of living was skyrocketing. We found that we were spending almost twice as much time as before shopping for basic supplies such as food and fuel. Our local African friends could no longer afford to buy their staple rice. They began relying on other sources of food, such as growing potatoes.

Later that summer, in August, we returned to the capital for our PBT team meetings. Our team was growing, with over forty people gathered for a week. The children enjoyed being together with their friends, and Jim and I enjoyed the fellowship of our colleagues.

Even though the growth in our team and family was a blessing, living with that many people in a cramped space for a week was stressful. Our family of six was packed into a tiny guest room, with kids on air mattresses on the floor. About 30 boxes of groceries and other supplies we had purchased to take back up country were piled up in every empty floor space of our room.

It was hot and muggy at the peak of the rainy season, and we slept dripping with sweat all night. Jim dreaded shopping for four months of supplies and then trying to fit everything into our truck or onto our roof rack in the pouring rain. Jim began to have back pain like I had. I noticed he was getting testy and snappy with the kids in every situation. This was uncharacteristic of him.

As I had the opportunity once more to meet with another counselor and continue working through my issues, I suggested Jim meet with him as well. To his relief, Jim found the meetings extremely helpful. He'd been holding everything together for me for so long that he overlooked how the stress and trauma had impacted him. Jim was diagnosed with clinical depression and started on medication.

At one point, we met together with the counselor. It was clear that we needed a change. The counselor helped us to see that maybe leaving the mission field was what we needed to feel like we could begin living again and thriving. He told us we had a choice. This gave us a sense that we finally had permission to leave if that was best for our family to heal. We did not have to stay in this place that was wounding us. Getting out might be the answer.

Africa had taken its toll on both my physical and mental health and Jim's as well. We realized that maybe we needed more than just a furlough or temporary home assignment to heal. We needed a season. As Jim and I prayed together, we realized that leaving Africa for a season, or perhaps for good, was the direction we needed to go. It initially made us uncomfortable since we had lived this way for so long and couldn't remember anything else. But we began to feel it was the right decision for this phase of our life. I needed to leave formal ministry where there were no expectations. Jim needed a place to continue working on the translation project, free from trauma, chaos, and distraction.

Our counselor helped us to cast a vision for how this next phase of our lives might look. We began to find hope and momentum as we formulated a plan where Jim could continue the translation project in the US remotely, just as we had planned to do during our evacuation period. Many of our teams were doing this. They also experienced health problems that made living in West Africa without good medical care difficult. With modern internet technology, remote Bible translation was possible.

I looked closely at my life over the next several months to uncover who I really was and why my struggle had been so difficult. With my counselor's help, I was able to figure out a lot of things. Deep down inside, I had to face my conflicting emotions. Part of me felt obligated to live out what I had believed was my calling since the age of eleven. The other part of me wanted to leave formalized ministry altogether. I struggled with the idea of leaving Africa. Didn't Jesus call all of us to fulfill the great commission? If we left, would we be disobeying God? What would our supporting churches think? What would we do? Who would we be?

From the time I was eleven, I had idolized many missionaries and aspired to be like them. I held to an ideal model of what success would look like. Their success had become the measure of my own success, even my identity. When my ministry in West Africa began to play out, it didn't look like I expected. There were some great achievements and victories, to be sure. But why didn't it feel like enough? After 18 years in this work, why did I feel like such a failure? I wasn't as strong as I thought I would be. People back home may have looked up to me, but inside I didn't feel worthy of it.

As Jim and I worked through our struggles, we realized that perhaps we had allowed our identities to be found too much in *what* we did and *where* we served rather than in *whose* we were. I began asking myself, "Have I wrapped up my identity in being a missionary more than being in Christ? Had I measured my success by comparing myself and my ministry to others?"

One of the resources the counselor gave us was a book by Parker Palmer, *Let Your Life Speak*. Palmer pointed out that trying to live someone else's life will invariably fail and may even do great damage. When we force ourselves into a mold that was not meant for us, we violate the true self God intended us to be, sometimes at great cost. He said there is a great gulf between our true selves and how our egos want to be identified, with their protective masks and fictitious scenarios. He shares a quote from Rabbi Zusya, who said as an old man, "In the coming world, they will not ask me: 'Why were you not Moses?' They will ask me: 'Why were you not Zusya?'" [1]

Brent Curtis and John Eldredge in *The Sacred Romance* also spoke to this point. They argued that we have learned from parents and peers, at school, at work, and even from our spiritual mentors that something else is wanted from us other than our hearts. As young people, we inadvertently use others' voices and expectations to fit ourselves into their slots as we define our identity. We feel accomplished and complete when we have degrees or titles behind our names. We are trained to conform to a norm. Often, driven by fear, we betray our true selves to gain others' approval. As a result, we often find ourselves doing the right thing for the wrong reasons.[2] This was where we were. We sensed for a long time that we needed to leave but were afraid of what others might think. So instead, we carried on, living out others' expectations of us.

We learned another truth about ourselves: too easily, we can hide in Christian service. Satan whispers to us that performance is more important. We do things, even noble things, that may look good to us for a while. But eventually, we distort ourselves and our relationship with the Father. In *Telling Secrets*, Frederick Buechner says we often try to make ourselves into something that we hope the world will like better than our original selves. In the process of living out that story, the original self gets buried so deep that most of us will end up not living out our true selves at all.[3] The reality is we are each created uniquely with a purpose, and we reach our fullest potential when we surrender to what God wants to do in us and through us in the way he designed. That doesn't look the same for everyone. The question for me was, what was God really wanting to do in me and through me?

Another thing we worked through was our sense of calling. In his book *When Your World Falls Apart*, Dr. David Jeremiah shared the story of his friend, Dr. John Hovey, a surgeon, who developed Parkinson's disease. As he slowly lost control of his hands, he began to see how this impacted his work as a surgeon. Dr. Hovey realized he would eventually lose his ability to do what he did best: operate. But more than that, he realized he would lose the affirmation of those he treated. So, he asked himself, "Is my identity as a doctor more important than my identity as his disciple?" [4]

Similarly, the thought of not being a missionary anymore was scary to Jim and me. We had been doing it for so long it had become our identity. If that identity was stripped away, who were we? What would we do? We learned that our Christian culture too often labels our missionary service or vocation in any other field as our "calling." By nature, we tend to take on that vocation as an identity. We then measure our performance and worth based on what people typically perceive that vocation requires. When that vocation is ripped away, we feel like failures and become insecure in our identities.

Our counselor helped us see that an honest appraisal of Scripture will demonstrate that God's will for us and our true "calling" is to salvation in Christ, holiness, righteousness, loving others with a Christlike love, and sharing the hope we have with the world. With that comes sharing the Gospel wherever we are and in whatever way God has uniquely gifted us and provided us opportunities to do so. God's specific will for me is not a dot but more like an umbrella. God gives us choices under that umbrella as long as we adhere to his moral will, which is specifically spelled out in Scripture. There might be multiple paths that one can take and still remain within God's will. We must choose prayerfully based on our motives, preferences, talents, gifts and abilities, and advice from trusted counsel. No choice is a guarantee for success. Most choices, even good choices, will come with adversity. How we respond with continued faith amid adversity is where God holds us accountable. [5]

When our sense of calling and identity are defined in this way, no trauma, culture stress, thwarted plans, unfulfilled dreams, disillusionment, loss, military coup, pandemic, change in career, health status, or any other circumstances will shake us from fulfilling our true calling. Nor will our identity be shaken. Our calling and identity must never be tied to a particular place, mission field, career, title, role, or even people group, but rather to Christ alone and to faithfulness to him. That looks different for each of us in our unique journey with him. Our roles may change through the seasons of life, but our identity should remain firmly rooted in him.

I began to see that I needed to strip away the missionary title and simply be his disciple, leaning on him alone to find my true self. My true calling, first and foremost, was to remain faithful to him, not to a place or to a role. The journey he laid out for me involved suffering and many trials. My job was to persevere in believing, despite what life threw my way. Many times in my journey, I could have been tempted to *"curse God and die,"* as Job's wife counseled him to do.[6] But I didn't. I chose to respond as Job did, *"The LORD gave and the LORD has taken away; may the name of the LORD be praised."*[7] I knew, above all, that I had no other hope. As the Apostle Peter told Jesus, *"Lord, to whom shall we go? You have the words of eternal life."*[8]

I wanted to know the true meaning of finding my significance in Christ and let that be enough. I prayed to God that would be enough. I decided that pursuing him was all that mattered. Maybe, in time, God would rekindle a passion for ministry in me.

As I came to this new understanding, I had to refine my theology. I had believed being a missionary in the traditional sense was the center of God's will for me and, therefore, the safest place to be. The reality was that it was a dangerous place. Safety, security, and comfort were never guaranteed nor promised. In fact, as I searched the Scriptures, I found that the truth was quite the opposite. Jesus said to take up our cross daily and follow him.[9] Not a pretty, polished metal cross hanging on a chain, but rather the horrific, ugly cross on which Jesus suffered and died. Following Jesus meant suffering and even death for many of his first disciples and for countless others throughout history. Why should I expect to get the penthouse suite?

My upbringing in a sheltered and privileged American culture had shaped and distorted my view of who God was and what following Christ meant. I was raised in a culture where young girls dreamed of being princesses who would someday be swept off their feet by Prince Charming and live happily ever after if they did everything just right. And even though I knew that many missionaries throughout history had suffered and even paid the ultimate price, my faith had somehow been shaped by the idea that God would bless and protect me if I did everything right. My unmet expectations were driving my anxiety.

This understanding brought me tremendous freedom and release from anxiety. I had believed that service on a foreign mission field was the highest calling and anything less was unacceptable. But as my mental and physical health declined, I felt tormented with the guilt of not measuring up. With counseling, I began to see that I was wounded and in need of healing. The impact of the things that had happened to me was significant. Some wounds caused scars. Others caused disability. I now had to learn to navigate life with both.

As I wrestled with where to go from here, I recognized that the interests and talents I had set aside in order to go to the mission field were not in moral conflict with God's will. God had put these gifts inside me like his signature on my life, screaming to be heard. When I denied them, a part of me died. My gifts had a purpose; if I did not express them, then part of God's work he chose to reveal in me and through me would be silenced. What's more, God uses us in many ways through different seasons of our lives. Was I trying to write my own story rather than let God shape it into what he wanted it to be, wounds and all? The challenge

I now faced was to allow God to use me and shape me in new ways that I had not planned.

As we returned to our home and resumed our translation work up country, I found solace in my garden, seeing God in even the smallest creature or flower. What a gift he had given! I planted a new vegetable garden and found joy in painting again, taking back the simple pleasures of using my interests and talents to connect with God, one thing at a time. Exercising the discipline of celebrating the simple things helped me slowly regain my joy and get my life back. I didn't want to end up becoming a victim of my life; I wanted to find purpose and meaning in it. I found ways to use these gifts to bless others. We played with our children, and I found greater joy in keeping my home. Mother Theresa once said, *"Be faithful in small things because it is in them that your strength lies."*[10] So too, these simple things strengthened me.

We continued to enjoy sweet fellowship with our colleagues. Jim continued to plug away on the translation project. He finalized the revision of the book of Exodus, prepared a special printing of Matthew and Genesis, and began to work on Psalms. Jim's depression continued for about three months. But with the counselor's encouragement, he began exploring writing, a hidden talent that seemed to give him the drive to carry on.

One night I dreamed of being at a huge banquet, maybe in a church reception hall, but I wasn't sure. A handsome Italian chef had orchestrated it. He had all his invited guests sit down wherever they wanted. As I was about to sit down, something told me to go to another place where no one was sitting. Then the chef began handing out balloons. I was one of the first ones to get a balloon, and I immediately noticed that mine was covered with wedding symbols. I suddenly realized our host had chosen me as his bride. I swelled with the joy of being the chosen one. I woke from this dream sensing that God had shown me a side of

his love for me: I was not second best; I wasn't "less than" because I failed
to be the perfect missionary. He loved me for who I was. I didn't have to
prove anything. He chose me and delighted in me.

On another night, I went to bed struggling – disappointed with
people who had let me down in a particular situation. For a short
moment, a past wound was reopened. As I tried to fall asleep that night,
my anxiety kept growing and kept me from sleeping. I cried out to God
to speak to me and let me hear his voice instead of the unhelpful voice
inside my head. Suddenly, a deep, restful sleep came over me. I sensed
that God was inviting me to enter his rest and put my anxieties aside.

As we pressed on during the next few months, we set a tentative field
departure date for a year. We wanted ample time to bring closure to our
African lives at our own pace, without regrets. We made a plan to visit
the remaining teams up country. This would allow us to finish Jim's role
as the mission director for language programs.

The thought of leaving Africa after so many years brought on mixed
emotions. I had so many good memories but many difficult ones as well.
Leaving all that was familiar, even if it wasn't a healthy situation, was
hard to do. They say that you can leave Africa, but Africa never leaves
you. Africa had gotten under our skin. It was part of us, whether we
wanted it to be or not. It had changed us. Breaking free from that would
be difficult, but our old dream was dying and was being replaced by a
new one. Now in our mid-40s, we both felt like we were going through
a midlife crisis of sorts. In reality, we were entering a new season.

As we looked toward the future dream, it still seemed far off. Yet, in
some ways, we felt entombed during our wait. We had cast a future vision
and laid it into our heavenly Father's hands, trusting that he would guide
us through the uncertainty. We had found the courage to move into
another unknown, stepping out boldly even if it didn't fit the paradigm
others had for us.

Sitting down and making a list of the steps toward our goal was helpful. We had purchased the land in the US and were saving Jim's pension money to possibly build a house there someday. I prepared a resume for a nursing job. We drafted a letter to our supporters and made a budget. We sorted through our things and began sending back mementos and other treasured items with visitors from the US. Other belongings we sold or gave away.

In the fall of 2008, answers to some long-standing prayers refreshed us. For two years now, I had suffered from ringing in my ears and dizziness, which my doctor had said was Meniere's disease. So many times, the roar in my ear was unrelenting. I severely restricted my diet to battle it. I lost sleep and often stayed in bed half the day from the overwhelming dizziness. At times I burst into tears over it. Every night my husband and children would pray the same prayer, "Help mommy's ear to get better." Then suddenly, I went a whole week without symptoms. The week turned into a month, then two months, until the symptoms were eventually gone altogether. In many ways, I felt like I had my life back.

Another matter of prayer was our internet service. The connection had been poor for months, impeding much of Jim's work. Jim spent hours every day just trying to resolve the problems with the phone company. One day the phone lines finally got fixed, and our connection was restored. At the same time, Jim's two-month-old computer problems were resolved, allowing him to make progress once again.

Additionally, our night guard stopped showing up for work regularly, leaving us and our home unprotected in a crime-ridden city. Our backup guard had taken a job with someone else, and we were left without options. For six days, we prayed that God would bring us someone reliable. On the seventh day, our neighbor Aliyou showed up looking for work. Grateful for a job, he agreed to our terms with no questions asked.

Just two months prior, Aliyou's wife had suffered a severe case of malaria, leaving her in a vegetative state for weeks. She had become bedridden and unresponsive. Her family had stopped feeding her. Neighbors and friends said she had a demon and was being punished for having an adulterous relationship with her brother-in-law. I began visiting her, laying hands on her, and praying over her. I read to her about how Jesus healed people and cast out demons. I counseled her family on how to conduct therapy exercises on her and feed her. I encouraged Aliyou to be gentle with her, forgive her, and show her the love she needed. I told the women caring for her to stop talking ill of her, especially in her presence, and that they needed to speak words of life and healing to her.

About a week after we hired Aliyou, he asked me to come to his house and see his wife again. I had not seen her in two weeks and feared the worst. But, instead, there she was, sitting up, getting up by herself, and talking. She smiled at me and thanked me. I praised God for not only healing her but giving me hope and a reminder that he was still at work and in control.

In November, we took a long trip to several remote village locations to visit colleagues. As the PBT language programs director, Jim counseled and encouraged other members of our larger team. It was a breath of fresh air for me to get away from our town, visit other colleagues, share our victories and struggles, and give our children more opportunities to enjoy fellowship with other English-speaking kids. Traveling through parts of the country where I had worked years before was bittersweet. It brought back fond memories, but I realized this would probably be the last time, and I may never return. The trip felt like a farewell tour. As I walked around greeting people in the villages where our colleagues worked, the fact that our remaining time in Africa was short began to hit me. I laughed with the people, shared their food, and tried to embrace the moments.

Unfortunately, I became very ill with some intestinal bug while on that trip and ended up severely dehydrated in bed for two days. I wondered if it was that little sip of mystery soup one of the villagers had offered me. On top of that, my back pain had seriously flared up because of the long, bumpy roads. I could barely move without severe pain. Nevertheless, I endured the roads with all the strength and character I could muster before crashing into bed at night, completely exhausted.

I remembered my enthusiasm and adventure the first time I traveled up country eighteen years earlier, excited at the opportunity of roughing it in the African bush. Almost two decades later, that romantic notion had utterly lost its allure as I lay there sick, suffering back pain, dehydration, and disorientation. As so many times before, I feared I was going to die. Whether the medication I took helped or not, God mercifully restored my health. However, from then on, there was a sharp pain in my stomach that would not subside and would continue for the next two years until I got a proper diagnosis.

We left that location to visit another family whose primary role was to take the Scriptures we translated and carry them by foot into remote areas of the country. Jim with his prosthetic leg, and I with my bad back, were impressed how God had equipped us to translate but not to do the task our colleagues were doing. They and their team would often trek for weeks upon end by foot across rough terrain, counting on God to direct them to *"houses of peace."* [11] These hosts would welcome them in, feed them, and receive the Good News with open hearts.

Because of our physical limitations, we knew trekking was someone else's job. God had given each of us a different role to play in his bigger picture. We could see the beauty of his plan, how he uses many members of one body, each person equipped to do a different task, as the Apostle Paul explained. Yet he warned us to think of ourselves *"with sober judgment."* [12] As much as I wanted to be the story's heroine, I was terribly inadequate and inserted myself in God's way far too often. As we planned to embark on our journey to find our new "normal" US life, I prayed that God would continue to work through me to bring glory to himself, not me.

After returning home from our trip, we prepared to celebrate Christmas with our immediate family and some of our newest colleagues in town. Unfortunately, a military coup took place in our host country two days before Christmas. Things remained calm for a few days but then began to heat up. Constant automatic gunfire throughout one particular night made it difficult to sleep. Our youngest children were crying and scared, and our older two were concerned and were asking lots of questions. Our night guard was sick that night and couldn't come to work, so we were a little more uneasy than usual, as our home was unprotected. We tried to get through the night, hoping for the best. The following day, our new colleagues discovered a bullet had gone through their roof, barely missing their computer. Our solar panels were not so fortunate.

We tried to celebrate Christmas and carry on with normal activities amidst intermittent gunfire. I treated burn patients, took down Christmas decorations, packed things for the US, and tried to get some schooling done with the kids. I prayed, prepared our food, and cleaned our home. We wanted to monitor the situation and communicate with friends and family back home, but we couldn't get a good internet connection because communication services had become restricted due to the coup.

After several days of trying to carry on everyday life under these conditions, my brain became foggy and began to shut down. All the uncertainty wearied me. Plus, I had forgotten to take my thyroid meds multiple times, which made things worse.

I noticed a pattern of brain fog emerging every time there was any crisis: even multi-tasking would trigger it. I would get confused and forgetful and was unable to process anything. There were days I forgot to fix lunch. I feared the family might starve to death if I didn't get my act together. I took little power naps throughout the day to clear my head. I realized that a simpler life, free from chaos, was what I needed most of all right now to find rest for my soul and clear my mind. I prayed God would grant us that in the New Year.

As January marched along, I felt restless, wishing our targeted departure date of August would arrive soon. I wanted a quick fix but realized he was asking me to endure the desert journey of waiting. My thoughts went to our papaya trees. They seemed to sprout everywhere, wherever the seeds fell. They were one of the fastest-growing trees in our yard, shooting up quickly in the heavy rainy season, often bearing fruit in the first year. However, their wood was soft and airy. After five years, the trees usually fell over, their roots too shallow and the trunk too weak to bear the weight of the heavy fruit.

The papaya tree reminded me of my own spiritual growth and healing. Growth that took place too fast would not last or allow me to endure more crises. I needed time to grow my roots slowly and deeply, with time to rest and form a sturdy trunk before more hardship arose. In Mark 4, Jesus talked about how the farmer plants grain, which grows on its own *"though he does not know how."* [13] I needed to allow God to grow me at his own pace, wait patiently for his timing in everything, and trust his methods.

At the same time, I didn't want to miss the moment. Every day presented its challenges, so I focused on thankfulness once again. I looked for small accomplishments. In school, I rejoiced when all the kids did their assignments well. Six-year-old Aisha was finally reading that word she had been struggling with for weeks. Joshua finished school before 3 p.m. for a change and embarked on a new creative outlet: working on a stop-motion movie he wanted to try his hand at. Katie put aside her frustration with her little siblings long enough to read them a story, and

Gabriel and Aisha took delight in hearing Dr. Seuss read over and over again. Even though the meat grinder was acting up, I rejoiced that our freezer was full of ground beef. I was thankful that I could prepare a healthy meal on time and that I had all the ingredients.

I watched through the louvered glass of our kitchen window as my children played together in our garden, laughing, chasing each other, swinging, running, and enjoying their youthfulness without a care in the world. Their familiar days playing in that garden would soon be no more. I cherished the moment. I wondered if they would grow to love the new place as they had loved this one. I de-cluttered our house, purging unnecessary stuff to make our eventual move easier. In this process, I pictured all this work would hopefully lead us to a simpler life.

I realized that living out what God had put in front of me – to live for the day – was a success. It didn't seem like much then, but over the long haul, I knew it would amount to something much bigger than I could see from my limited vantage point. I reflected on the words of James 1:17, *"Whatever is good and perfect comes down to us from God our Father."*[14] God's good gifts were evident if I looked for them.

Chapter Twenty-Two

A SURPRISE DEPARTURE

"The Lord will watch over your coming and going, both now and forever more." (Psalm 121:8 NIV)

A fter the new government had seized power, the new president commissioned soldiers to reclaim government-owned property illegally sold to citizens over the previous several decades by corrupt officials in the preceding regime. There were rumors of bulldozers leveling houses in the capital and people being evicted from their homes in the middle of the night. Such reports seemed like a distant threat since they were not occurring in our area.

With five months left before our planned departure from Africa, we made every effort to enjoy fellowship with our missionary community while we still could. One particular weekend in April, we hosted an out-of-town family and were relaxing under the shade trees in our courtyard. Suddenly there came a loud pounding on our gate. Jim opened it, and several soldiers, police officers, and government officials walked into the yard.

One of the officials spoke up. "This house was built on government property and is now being reclaimed by the new government."

As he made the announcement, a soldier with a can of red paint marched up to our house and painted two big red crosses on it, marking it as government property. This was beyond disturbing.

Their visit lasted about fifteen minutes. Some of them marched around our place, following the guy with the paint can. Others just milled about. We asked them what all this meant for us.

"This is government property that was illegally developed, so you will have to leave. You can take your questions to the district governor's office."

The same entourage visited most of our immediate neighbors, giving them the same ultimatum. We could hear wailing from every direction as our African friends grieved the impending loss of their homes.

In shock, we wondered what we should do next. Jim, our African co-translator, and I went to the district governor's office the following day. We hoped to ask him if we would really be required to move out. Doing so would ruin our plans to leave the house and many of our things for another missionary family scheduled to arrive later that year. Jim feared we would get the false-assurance type of answer typical of our host culture.

A soldier escorted us into a room outside the district governor's office, where we waited for some time. When we were finally ushered into his office, instead of the governor with whom Jim had chatted on several occasions, we were introduced to the army general who had replaced him.

Jim explained our dilemma, "A group of soldiers and government agents came to our home, painted red crosses on all the buildings, and said that we need to leave. We have lived here for twelve years. Are we really required to move out of our home?"

When the general began talking, it became clear that he was drunk on power. I could feel the tension rising inside me as he described with contempt how the previous regime illegally sold government land.

He continued on, punctuating every statement with beady, shifting, maniacal glances.

"If the new president commanded me to kill my own brother, I would do it. Whatever the new president wants, he gets."

At that moment, it dawned on us that we were standing in the presence of a crazed warlord. I felt uneasy, and fear grew inside me.

He finally answered our question, "We aren't going to make you leave, but you should go."

I was distraught as we left his office. I felt the need to rush home, pack our bags, and leave as quickly as possible. Though equally alarmed at the general's demeanor, Jim was actually relieved we had gotten an honest answer. For Jim, our course of action was crystal clear.

We went home, informed our guests of the meeting's outcome, and started to lay out a plan. We didn't know how much time we had, but we knew that the sooner we got out, the better. It hit us that our departure from Africa had arrived. It now seemed futile to wait the remaining four months. It was hard to wrap my brain around the reality of it. Everything seemed to be happening so fast. I couldn't help but ask God why. But I knew by now nothing had to make sense. I had to simply trust God. One thing I did realize: everything we had done to prepare to leave thus far, both emotionally and physically, had prepared us better for this moment, though it caught us by surprise.

We planned to pack up, sell as much as we could, and store the rest at a colleague's house. We would head toward the coast in hopes of flying back to the US after our team meetings scheduled later that month. We informed our mission leadership, who began purchasing tickets for us.

Over the next few days, we sorted through every piece of clothing, toy, bead, trinket, kitchen gadget, piece of paper, library book, memorabilia, and anything else we had, and decided what to do with it. I had never before imagined trying to have a yard sale in Africa, but we decided to give it a try. We put everything out and informed the neighbors. They came in droves, eager to buy everything from plastic ware to furniture at dramatically reduced prices. A few fights broke out between neighbors or local children vying for their right to have even our trash.

Fellow missionaries from all over the region and other organizations came to help us disassemble, pack up, sort through, prioritize, and move 16 truckloads of furniture and other items. We had a few refreshing moments – a cold soda, a laugh here and there, a walk down memory lane, and friends at our side. One of the hardest things for our kids was to say goodbye to their pets. Despite this, they were real troopers and maintained a positive attitude through it all. We did our best to make the circuit around town to say our last farewells to our African neighbors and friends that we had come to know over the years.

Eight days later, we were completely moved out, packed, and ready to leave for the coast the next day. We were exhausted. Before leaving the house, I made one last run into town to get some supplies. In town, a police officer pulled me over and began yelling at me, telling me I had committed some driving infraction. I had no reserve left. I started sobbing openly at his affront. Several passersby scolded the officer, telling him to leave me alone. Couldn't he see the poor white woman was upset?

We spent our final night in town at a fellow missionary's home. Jim laid down on his stomach on the hard tile floor and passed out from exhaustion. His hands were black with dust and dirt. I tried to sleep in a strange bed. My back was killing me, my legs were stiff, and my whole body was aching. My ears were ringing, and my head was spinning. We had been through some of the hardest days yet. We had gotten through some tough times before, and I knew we would get through this too. God was with us.

I was reminded that we are merely sojourning on this earth and that our true home is in heaven. It was nearly Easter. I thought about the Resurrection, and it filled me with hope during this time of uncertainty and turmoil, giving me the strength to press on. We were thankful that the moving out was now behind us.

We drove out of town the next day, pressing forward to what lay ahead. We were so worn out, and we both felt ourselves becoming ill. By the time we arrived in the capital, Jim was so sick that he could not unload the car. Thankfully several missionary friends were waiting there to help us. The next day we took medicine, got some rest, and began to feel better. Over the next week, we enjoyed the outpouring of love from our colleagues who went the extra mile for us, helping in every conceivable way. We felt truly blessed by the body of Christ ministering to us.

On April 30th, 2009, after 19 years of serving in Africa, I boarded a plane with my family and left the African continent for the last time. We knew there was no turning back. We left our home of 12 years, the only home our children had ever really known, and the pets, the friends, the ministry, and the memories.

Finally, after 30 hours of transit, we arrived safely in the US with all our luggage. The many friends and family who met us at the airport and helped us transport our baggage and family members home were a huge blessing. Over the next few days, we rested, unpacked, got our bearings, and recovered from the jetlag and intestinal parasites we carried back as stowaways on the trip. My back seized up within days of our return, sending me to the ER in severe pain. Weeks of hauling boxes, furniture, and luggage had taken their toll.

.

Chapter Twenty-Three

OUT OF AFRICA

"How do you pick up the threads of an old life, how do you go on, and in your heart begin to understand, there is no going back? There are some things that time cannot mend, some holes that go too deep, they have taken hold." Frodo Baggins, The Return of the King.[1]

"For you, LORD, have delivered me from death, my eyes from tears, my feet from stumbling, that I may walk before the LORD in the land of the living." (Psalm 116:8-9, NIV)

The continent of Africa captured my imagination growing up. I had dreamed of living in Africa my whole life. I had the idea in my mind that Africa was this wild and beautiful place. And it was. When I first went to Africa, it was indeed beautiful. And wild. It fulfilled all my expectations.

And then it didn't. Eventually, Africa lost its romantic allure, and I saw another side to it. There were mosquitoes. Driver ants. Locusts. Droughts. Famines. Lack of electricity. Water shortages. Fuel shortages.

Sweltering heat. Nights covered in sweat without air conditioning or a fan. Rodents climbing over the bed at night. Bats in the rafters. Malaria, Ebola, and pointless death. Accidents. Tragedies. Dangerous, winding roads and unskilled drivers. Beggars playing on your emotions to get a quick buck, yet refusing any real help you offer them. Alcohol, drugs, thieves, riots, corrupt government officials, war, bombs, and crazed warlords. People suffering through unimaginable things. The devious exploiting the weak. There were sinful people – like you and me.

Sin has entered the world and entered the human heart everywhere. Everywhere, each culture has a unique spin on things, sometimes creating beautiful cultural practices, clothing, ways of preparing food, and customs. Yet deep in the heart of every culture are signs of a longing – a search for reconciliation with a Creator long forgotten. And there are also signs of rebellion against that Creator – evidence of a stubborn and defiant power struggle to dominate and wield control contrary to God's design. Sin and evil can be found everywhere – we can't escape them.

Over time, I saw Africa for what it really was, the good and the bad. I saw beautiful people living simple lives and struggling to survive. I saw that sin has seized the hearts and minds of some people in sometimes pretty ugly ways. Evil and tragedy occasionally spilled over and touched my colleagues, my family, and my life. We were not immune there any more than at home in the US. In Africa, I discovered a dark side of myself as well. I dreamed I would change the world and do heroic things. I naively imagined I would instantly bond with people there and connect with them. With some, I did, but at other times, I struggled to love the people the way God did. Africa was clearly not a walk in the park. But neither was the US.

Our transition back to the United States came with mixed emotions. On the one hand, we were free from the hassles of living cross-culturally in a developing, war-torn region of the world with shaky infrastructure.

On the other hand, we were re-entering a world that had changed dramatically. For our children, the transition meant leaving behind all that was familiar. Katie and I stopped to use the public restroom in one of the airport terminals. After I left, I noticed Katie hadn't followed me out. When I returned to find her, she stood at the sink staring at the running water and looking dismayed. I asked her what was wrong, and she said she couldn't figure out how to get the water to turn off. Automatic sensor faucets were a foreign concept to her. In our part of Africa, where water was often in short supply and had to be conserved, one would never walk away from a running faucet. I laughed and assured her that she would not get in trouble if she left the water running.

Driving on the paved highway for the first time, I commented how nice it was on my bad back not to bump around on dirt roads. My son Joshua, then 11 years old, asked innocently, "Do they have dirt roads in America, Mommy?" We laughed and told him, "Yes. There were dirt roads in the country, but not in the city." Another time in our first days back, we all laughed together at a sign outside of a construction site that said, "Caution, dirt on road." We all agreed that in Africa, the sign should read, "Caution, road is dirt!"

But beyond the obvious differences to our children, the US was clearly not the same country I had left nineteen years earlier. Just as in Africa, sin had continued to run amuck in its own way. An old adage says that if you drop a frog into a pot of hot water, the frog will jump out. However, if you put the frog in cool water and slowly bring it to a boil, it will stay in the water until it cooks to death. Away in Africa all those years, the warming water of gradual moral decay had invaded our home country. Many Americans seemed unaware of the water slowly simmering to a boiling point. It was like we had been placed in cryogenic sleep for two decades, then reawakened to a new world. The decline was subtle and less noticeable for those who lived here, but the changes shocked us.

We planned for Jim to continue the translation project remotely with our co-translator via electronic communication. However, we would not be able to survive on our limited mission budget; I would have to find a job to supplement our income. Within a few weeks, I filled a nurse position in a local emergency department. We made plans to join millions of other Americans in taking out a mortgage. We hoped to soon build a house on our country property.

I was finally able to get my gastrointestinal problems firmly diagnosed. First, my doctor told me I had the worst case of celiac disease he had ever seen; my small intestines were severely eroded, causing me to be malnourished. Then came the diagnosis of a diseased gall bladder and Barrett's esophagus, a pre-cancerous condition. Surgery and some radical changes to my diet over the next few years helped to resolve these issues enough to keep them in check. With persistent physical therapy, a healed gut, improved nutrition, and less stress, my back and joint problems improved dramatically.

As we adjusted to our new normal in the US, I could see that God had given us the gift of time to heal. At first, I had no desire to be involved in ministry. Ministry, after all, was where I was traumatized. People expected things from you and continually scrutinized you in ministry. I already felt like a failure. The last thing I wanted to do was help others because, at that moment, I needed to help myself. Our family was in transition and in survival mode. We were homeschooling our children. We had a house to set up. I had to work to help our family out financially. Staying busy was a good thing to help us get into a routine. But I had little emotional energy to engage in any sort of ministry.

Jim was different. We found a local church where he began to serve in various capacities. He also continued to work remotely with our African colleagues on the translation project.

One challenge in my battle with depression was my inability to tolerate anti-depressant medications. So, my journey back to health, at least in
the beginning, had to be done without drugs. It was not easy, but it was
possible. I relied on other options: rest, nutrition, vitamin supplements,
counseling, friends, God's Word, and prayer. And time. Although my
depression waned fairly quickly, the post-traumatic stress and anxiety
never completely subsided.

As I have walked through this journey, I have learned one very crucial
thing: to keep my eyes on Jesus. After Jesus miraculously fed over 5000
people one day, we read in Matthew 14 how Jesus sent his disciples in
their boat to go before him to the other side of the Sea of Galilee while
he dismissed the crowds. When evening came, Jesus was alone on the
shore. But by then, the boat was far away from land, beaten by the wind
and waves. As Jesus approached the boat during the fourth watch of the
night, he told the disciples, *"Take courage! It is I. Don't be afraid."* Even
though the wind and waves had not ceased, Jesus told them not to fear.[2]

Jesus had not yet calmed the raging sea. Instead, he indicated that
his presence was enough reason for them not to fear the danger around
them. Peter responded by saying, *"Lord, if it is you, command me to come
to you on the water."*

Jesus said, *"Come!"* Peter got out of the boat and walked on the water
toward Jesus. But when Peter became distracted by the wind and the
waves, he panicked and began to sink. I saw myself in Peter. In my early
college years, I was zealous to follow Jesus when he said, *"Come."* But
many times when danger came near, I took my eyes off Jesus long enough
to begin sinking. The waves distracted me. Some waves were huge, harsh,
and brutal, knocking me down.

Processing my traumatic experiences with a counselor was also crucial
in helping me to move toward healing. I realized that I needed to correct
some faulty theology that contributed to my anxiety. I once believed
that God would protect me from evil and danger. When he didn't, I felt

he had abandoned me. With time, I understood better what David was talking about in Psalm 23, *"Even though I walk through the darkest valley, I will fear no evil, for you are with me."*[3] I could now see that sometimes evil is a real threat and can harm us. Although God had delivered us from many dangers many times, and some of those we couldn't even see, there were times he did not. But this did not mean he had abandoned us. The real message of David's words that I somehow missed in my formative years was that *while in that valley,* he would be present.

He elaborates in verse 5: *"You prepare a table before me in the presence of my enemies."*[4] God didn't always remove the enemies, but instead, right there in front of the enemies, God was present, and his good gifts were provided in plain sight – a table abundantly overflowing with good things. God was walking with me *through the valley,* was present with me *in the presence of my enemies,* and provided for me abundantly in that moment. His presence would be my strength to endure it and even rejoice rather than succumb to fear. Jesus told his disciples on the boat that his presence was enough reason not to fear. He's got this. We need only to trust him. And what made Peter stop sinking? He fixed his eyes on Jesus.

As the writer of Hebrews reminds us, God promised never to leave us or forsake us. *"So we say with confidence, 'The Lord is my helper; I will not be afraid. What can mere mortals do to me?'"*[5] His presence gives us the power and strength to overcome our fear and do the impossible, as David said in Psalm 27:

"The LORD is my light and my salvation—whom shall I fear?
*   The LORD is the stronghold of my life—of whom shall I be afraid?*
When the wicked advance against me to devour me,
*   it is my enemies and my foes who will stumble and fall.*
Though an army besiege me, my heart will not fear;
*   though war break out against me, even then I will be confident."*[6]

I needed to constantly remind myself of these truths and keep my eyes fixed beyond the waves of the moment. When I know, ultimately, that God is there and in control and knows how the story ends, then I can trust him with the outcome and what he is doing.

Looking back at my life, I can see how I allowed fear to dominate my thoughts. Doing so caused my courage to dwindle like Peter focusing on the waves. I also recognize the role Satan has in this battle for our minds. The Apostle Paul reminds us in his letter to the Ephesians:

"For our struggle is not against flesh and blood, but against the rulers, against the authorities, against the powers of this dark world and against the spiritual forces of evil in the heavenly realms."[7]

Elsewhere, Paul warns us to pay attention that *"...Satan might not outwit us. For we are not unaware of his schemes."*[8]

The Apostle Peter also warns us:

"Be alert and of sober mind. Your enemy the devil prowls around like a roaring lion looking for someone to devour."[9]

Jesus warns us that Satan is the *"father of lies."*[10] When we believe the lies Satan tells us about ourselves, about what we dread most, and we give in to fear and despair, this distracts us from the truth, our hope, and our true identity. Knowing what I know about how my story ends, I can boldly approach him without fear. I can say, "I know what you're up to, and I'm not afraid of you. I know who I am and Whose I am."

Modern psychology uses cognitive therapy to help depressed and anxious patients recognize and correct deeply held false negative thinking patterns that contribute to depression. God's Word promotes the same remedy, like when Paul encourages us to *"be transformed by the renewing of your mind."*[11] We must constantly keep our thoughts in check by reminding ourselves of truths from God's Word. When people who are depressed embrace the truth about their situation and correct faulty thinking, it launches their journey to freedom from depression. In the same way, when we as believers embrace the truth God tells us, we are able to recognize the lies of Satan and our own faulty ways of thinking that keep us enslaved in fear.

Clinging to what I knew was true got me through some of my darkest moments of depression. As followers of Jesus, when we understand and fix our thoughts on the truth about who God tells us we are in Christ, how much he loves us, and the certainty of our future hope, we begin the journey toward freedom from fear and anxiety.

Depression and anxiety are states of disturbed peace. Satan is ruthless and desires God's glory and our allegiance, so he pours a lot of effort into bringing us down. He often uses circumstances to distract us and catch us off guard. That makes it easy for us to become mired in despair, hopelessness, and fear.

When we are not prepared, we react defensively, in fear. We need a battle plan: anticipating enemy attacks and preparing ourselves for the coming battle. How do we do that?

The Bible tells us that God gives us the tools/weapons we need to fight him. Paul tells us in Ephesians that if we are to stand against the devil's evil schemes, we need to use spiritual weapons and armor to fight the spiritual battle.[12] One of those weapons is God's truth. We must cling to what we know is true about ourselves, our situation, and what God has revealed in his Word.

Embedded within Paul's discourse about how to fight the battle is the underlying assumption that there *is* a battle. It started at the beginning when Satan entered the garden. Adam and Eve, as far as the Scriptures tell us, are the only humans that have ever known what it is truly like to experience heaven on earth, and they threw it all away for a lie. Every attempt on our part to recreate that heaven on earth sets us up for failure. Believing the lie of Satan that life can be perfect here leads to suffering, disappointment, and heartache. Our unrealistic dreams leave us disappointed and unprepared for the war that is still raging. Instead of readying ourselves for battle, we numb ourselves with the pursuit of pleasures. We become distracted in constructing our kingdoms. And when our kingdoms fall, we wonder what hit us. Instead, we should have been making a battle plan all along.

There have been times I was better at waging this spiritual battle than at other times. When stress became overwhelming and unexpected traumatic events hit me like rapid-fire, those were when it was hardest to deflect the arrows. In those moments, I learned I needed to lean heavily into him and his Word and hold on tight until the onslaught passed. Sometimes, I simply had to hold up my shield of faith, another piece of armor, until the arrows stopped coming. Ultimately, leaning into him and holding on to my faith kept me from giving in to total despair during those terrifying experiences. Holding on to him, my sturdy rock, kept me from following through and acting on suicidal thoughts based on lies Satan told me. And as the storm passed, I was still found standing.

In the battle for my mind, God graciously orchestrated events that pulled me out of my dark place. As I picked up the pieces and navigated my new life in the US, I began encountering other souls battered by the storms of life. Walking with them through their pain, I forgot my own troubles and gradually experienced a new level of growth and healing. And this became an unexpected twist in my story.

Chapter Twenty-Four

NOTHING WASTED

As I settled into my new role in the US as an emergency department nurse, one thing that caught my attention was the alarming number of suicidal patients and drug overdoses. In the emergency
department, our team often attempted to resuscitate patients who had
overdosed. Unfortunately, some didn't make it.

As I worked in this new environment where so many were without
hope, God began to slowly transform my heart. Before I went to Africa, I
avoided some of these people. Now, here they were at my doorstep every
day. Their struggle with life was real. My own journey through depression, anxiety, and PTSD helped me better understand that struggle.

I remember one man in particular. He was stout, strong, and covered
in tattoos. He wore a leather jacket and sported long hair and beard –
the kind of guy your mother would have told you to avoid at all costs.
He resisted his police escort with every move as they brought him in
to determine if he was fit for confinement. He reeked of alcohol
and shouted obscenities at everyone that crossed his path. He was a
wife-beater. You could feel the tension in the nurse's station, comprised
primarily of female nurses, some of whom were divorced from wife
beaters and drunks. The hatred was palpable. All the other nurses said,
"Not it," as the officers sat him down in one of the exam rooms and cuffed
him to the bed rail.

But for some reason, when I looked at this man, I felt differently than they did. I could relate to him. Not because of what he had done but because of the struggle I sensed he felt. I gladly volunteered. The other nurses just shook their heads at me, like I was foolish and naïve and would soon learn how rough these types could be. The officers feared letting me be in the room with the man alone. But I wasn't afraid. Usually, I would have been. But not this time. I felt alive and on fire. Undaunted. I needed to talk to this man.

I approached him and spoke calmly as I took his blood pressure. I noticed a tattoo as I assessed his arm for a site to start an IV.

"What does this tattoo mean to you?" I asked.

His tone of voice calmed. "I got that when I was in Vietnam."

Vietnam. There it was. The trauma of my own "Vietnam" experience came to mind.

I pressed him for more information. "Were you traumatized in Vietnam?"

He looked up at me, and tears started forming in his eyes. He began to tell me what he experienced and how no one understood him, not even his wife, which is why they had so many conflicts. For years he had bottled it up inside and felt so alone and misunderstood. I reassured him that what he went through was awful and that I understood. I told him briefly about how I, too, had been traumatized by events in Africa. I understood PTSD. I knew he could not see a way out of the pit he was in. I knew what that felt like. I told him there was hope, that God loves him deeply, and that God is the God of second chances and forgiveness. I told him there was even hope of being reconciled with his wife.

Sitting in that emergency room with this leather-clad drunk, I finally realized that my trauma had meaning and purpose. It was as if I was suddenly pulled back to see a larger view of my life – seeing the entire forest rather than just the trees – and what God was doing all along. Perspective is everything. And I had no regrets. This was my purpose: I was the one for the job. My journey through fear all those years in Africa was on-the-job training. I finally got it.

As I left the room, the man thanked me. He was cooperative with all the staff after that. The officers looked at me in disbelief. The other nurses asked, "What did you do?" I told them I simply listened and let him tell his story. In no way was I excusing his abusive behavior. I just knew a human was in there somewhere, one that had been wounded and didn't know any other way to respond.

A year or so later, I had the opportunity to meet this man again. He was sober and cheerful. He was walking hand-in-hand with his wife. She was all smiles. He recognized me and, in a very gentle voice, he told me, "Thank you. You were right. I would never have believed it, but you were right." He told me it was the one thing that made everything start turning around for him.

I cannot tell you how many suicidal, overdosed, depressed, dying, and hurting people I have encountered as a nurse in the US over the past 14 years since we returned from Africa. The number of occasions is staggering. God has given me divine appointments with many of them. As a result, my perspective on ministry has broadened.

The truth is, every person we encounter is a mission field. As Christians, we are called to *people*, not places. The journey is not about us, but about connecting hurting people with God's redemptive plan. Life's struggles are real for everyone. We are called to incarnational ministry like Jesus, who became flesh and lived among us. We are called to be Jesus to people who suffer greatly in ways we often cannot understand. When we have the privilege to walk in their world, sometimes we get a taste of that world, even with its cruelty and harsh ways.

Experiencing those hardships gives us empathy, a deeper understanding of their pain, and insights into how God can use us to walk alongside them in their suffering and ultimately give them hope. We are

"Jesus with skin on," as one of my old professors once said, making God's presence in their life felt.

Several years later, one of the women in our church was found by her husband after a suicide attempt and taken to a nearby hospital. Her husband came to Jim and me, asking for help. After she was released from the hospital, we invited them to our home. I pulled the wife aside, prayed with her, and shared my story with her. After that, the four of us began meeting weekly. Not knowing where else to start, we began working through a book on gaining freedom from depression. Gradually we added biblical principles.

A few weeks later, another lady in the church came to mind while I was driving to work. I called her and encouraged her to attend our Freedom from Depression meeting. She came and brought along a friend who was also suffering. Our little group began to grow. Others joined one by one. Together we formed a small, safe, parish community where grief and struggles could be shared, emotions processed, and healing could take place.

The Freedom from Depression support group continued for many years. Other opportunities also came along, like leading Bible studies on coping with anxiety with a regional women's group and becoming a team member of a Grief Share support group in a local church. It was clear that God could redeem my worst experiences and use them for good. And I knew he promised to do just that, as the Apostle Paul says, *"And we know that in all things God works for the good of those who love him, who have been called according to his purpose."*[1]

In Africa, there was a particular wild lily that was so beautiful and intricate that I had hoped to add it to my collection. It was tough to find because it bloomed only one day a year. Finally, one day while our family was on an outing in a remote area, I found one in bloom. Excited, I dug it up, took it home, and planted the bulb in my garden. I added compost around it and watered it faithfully, along with all the other plants in my garden, but it would not sprout.

Finally, the seasonal rains began. As the barometric pressure changed, a massive storm came, saturating the ground. The next morning, the lily was in full bloom, having sprouted overnight. It was perfectly formed and exquisite to behold. I was reminded how that perfection came out of the dirt, rotting compost, and manure. And only after the storm, rain, and change in pressure did that root sprout into a beautiful lily.

So it is with us. There is often refuse and dirt in our journey. Just as a seed must die before it can sprout into a beautiful plant, we must also die to ourselves, giving up our sinful nature to embrace what God wants for us before we can be reborn. We also have to die to our preconceived ideas about what our lives are going to look like. We have to relinquish control. Sometimes it takes pressure and storms to sprout and mature us into what we are meant to be. As the book of James tells us, we can have joy knowing the hard experiences test our faith and produce endurance. That endurance has its perfect result, like the flower. We must patiently let God finish what he is doing in us so that we can be mature and complete, not lacking anything.[2]

It is easy to lose sight of the bigger picture when we are in the thick of the hard times. We fail to see that perhaps God has something bigger and better in store for us that he can only do if we go through the trial we are facing. But we can be sure God has an amazing plan for us. He has a plan to prosper us and not to harm us.[3]

Like the prophet Jeremiah described, God is like a potter, reshaping us the way he wishes into a vessel of his own design.[4] Can the clay tell the potter how to shape it?[5] Of course not! And just as a potter must press hard into the clay so that it can be centered and then molded, there are seasons in our lives when we may feel pressed hard by God. The pressing may be painful, but God knows just the right amount of pressure needed to shape us and not harm us. Once we are centered in him, fully surrendered, he can finally make us into something useful. Being molded into what he wants us to be is sometimes messy.

Does this mean that God intentionally allows harm to come to us for his purposes? Not always, but sometimes yes. In Scripture, we see many examples. The Israelites turned away from God over and over, following after the gods of the surrounding nations. As a result, we read how God caused other nations to conquer Israel for a time as a way to discipline them and turn them back to Him. Sometimes God uses a form of suffering to get a person's attention or redirect the course of events, ultimately producing a good outcome. If Baalam's donkey had not pressed Baalam's leg against the wall, Baalam would have kept going to his destruction.[6] And Jim is confident that he would not have repented and opened up to God's transforming power without his motorcycle accident, where he lost his leg. As a loving father disciplines his children to set them back on course, God often allows us to endure drastic circumstances to correct our misguided paths.

Clearly, there are times when God punishes the sins of the wicked. We see that over and over throughout the Old Testament. This shows God's righteous and just nature. Unfortunately, we all too often assume that when bad things happen, God must be punishing us. But we know this is most often not the case, as Jesus pointed out in John 9:2-3 when his disciples asked about the blind man, "His disciples asked him, *'Rabbi, who sinned, this man or his parents, that he was born blind?' 'Neither this man nor his parents sinned,' said Jesus, 'but this happened so that the works of God might be displayed in him.'*"[7] We see Jesus saying this another time when his friend, Lazarus, was about to die. He said, "*This sickness will not end in death. No, it is for God's glory so that God's Son may be glorified through it.*"[8]

Other times we see that good people suffer because of the evil of others or simply because we live in a fallen world. But in these situations, God doesn't waste anything. We see so many times throughout Scripture how God used a desperate situation to bring him glory, or used it for some greater purpose. He redeems the situation. If Stephen hadn't been stoned, it is unlikely that Saul of Tarsus would have become Paul the Apostle, whose missionary travels to Europe and Asia resulted in countless lives being saved.[9] And without the persecution that followed Stephen's martyrdom, Phillip would not have fled to Samaria and shared the gospel there and with the Ethiopian Eunuch, traditionally credited for starting the first church in Africa.[10] God used the situations for his purposes.

No one can deny the beauty of God's redemptive plan in the story of Joseph. Joseph was betrayed by his brothers, sold into slavery, falsely accused, and thrown into prison. God used these circumstances to transform him into a humble leader who would save nations and his own family from a famine. Joseph himself declared to the brothers who betrayed him, *"So then, it was not you who sent me here, but God,"*[11] and, *"You intended to harm me, but God intended it for good to accomplish what is now being done, the saving of many lives."*[12] Likewise, the Apostle Paul recognized that God gave him his thorn in the flesh, whatever it was, to keep him humble.[13] My own father's death led me to choose to follow Jesus.

Sometimes when bad things happen, God may be keeping us from something worse. Like when the water pipes leaked, and my delay kept me from potentially getting killed in the market. Or when our colleagues were in a bad accident in the US, and therefore not in their village when rebels invaded the region. Four months after our traumatic departure from Africa, we learned that some suspicious men had come to the town where we had lived, looking specifically for us. It was later revealed they were suspected to be terrorists from an organization that was targeting Americans throughout West Africa. One man was arrested by local police for helping them. We realized that if the soldiers had not come that day in April and asked us to leave, we would still have been there when these men came intending to do us harm. We were thankful to God: what had been a traumatic departure for us was now a blessing in disguise.

God is sovereign, meaning he has his hand in everything. He does not necessarily cause everything but often allows them to happen in a world where we are given free will. He is still in control, redeeming even evil acts of others to draw people back to himself and for the good of his bigger plan. God's ways may seem cruel to many because they see the world through their limited human perspective. God knows and sees the larger view of history, why he created us, and where he wants us to arrive.

Ultimately, we must recognize the fact that even God did not stop the evil turn of events that played out that fateful day on Golgotha when Jesus suffered a horrific death on the cross. God in the flesh willingly experienced not only life as we experience it, with fears, grief, and temptations, but also the worst pain and torture known to mankind. He is able to empathize with our struggles. He knows our grief. He was angered at injustice, felt the emotions of loss, and agonized as he faced his impending sacrifice to the point he even sweat drops of blood. He faced rejection, betrayal, ridicule, and mockery. And it all was part of God's perfect plan to redeem us and give us hope to be freed from the Curse because of his great love for us.

I wish I could say that time healed all my wounds completely. It didn't. The years after our return to the US, the pain of all that had happened was still there, right under the surface. For the most part, I began to feel pretty *normal* emotionally, and the PTSD was packed away like in a box in the closet. But, occasionally, triggers would cause it to rear its ugly head when I least expected it. Like when my sixteen-year-old son found himself upside down in our truck in a ditch. Or the time I was subpoenaed to appear in court to testify against a child abuser who had abused a patient I took care of in the ER. Or the time I was falsely accused of something. Or when people we trusted betrayed us.

Any traumatic or stressful event, even vaguely similar to the trauma I had experienced in Africa or events from my childhood, could trigger the PTSD, the anxiety, and the panic attacks. I had to learn to deal with it because it wasn't going away on its own. I discovered that even though the traumatic events of Africa were behind me, hints of them were everywhere. I even found my heart racing once when a certain movie was playing on the TV – it was the same movie my kids were watching the day the soldiers came to our house.

PTSD is like a ticket that instantly takes you on a warp-speed journey to the dark place of your trauma, along with all of its fear, anxiety, depression, and other emotions. Even with the best intentions, prayer, and spiritual weapons in my arsenal, I realized I couldn't simply think my way out of it. The renewing of my mind would take time and work. Eleven years after our return to the US, we experienced two very trying years. Certain events during that time sent me into a tailspin again, causing me to seek out specialized trauma counseling and try a newer medication that worked for my anxiety and depression. New trauma treatment modalities, such as EMDR and brain spotting, were helpful.

I realize now that my reactions to these triggers are fragmented reminders of my brokenness and my need to continually lean into God. The greatest gift God wants to give us is more of himself. He wants to be first in our lives. Too many times, we make things other than God our idols: comfort, safety, a boyfriend, spouse, family, children, money, fame, success, independence, or pride. Clinging to these things only results in more anxiety. None of them can satisfy the longing, the thirst, that God-shaped hole in our hearts that was put in us from the beginning of Creation. Only God himself, our Father, our Creator, can fill that void. We were made to reflect his glory. Sometimes he brings things into our lives to remind us that anything else is a shaky foundation. Sometimes he must take something away from us to make us trust in him alone. For me, it was my sense of security and my physical and mental health. Over time, I've learned to let go of my expectations and idols.

I know that what God brought me through and is still doing in my life is working out his perfect plan to make me trust him, even when it doesn't make sense to my logical mind. I am not the same person as when I first went to Africa. My mind is different, broken in many ways from years of trauma and stress. But my understanding of God is deeper, and my faith is stronger.

I also see that God can use my pain and brokenness for good, for his purpose, when I choose to surrender. It is not the path I would have chosen. But it is, nonetheless, my story. His story.

Joni Erickson, a quadriplegic from a tragic accident in her teen years, described it well in her book *Diamonds in the Dust*:

"Shattered glass is full of a thousand different angles, each one picking up a ray of light and shooting it off in a thousand directions. That doesn't happen with plain glass, such as a jar. The glass must be broken into many pieces. What's true of shattered glass is true of a broken life. Shattered dreams. A heart full of fissures. Hopes that are splintered. A life in pieces that appears to be ruined. But given time and prayer, such a person's life can shine more brightly than if the brokenness had never happened. When the light of the Lord Jesus falls upon a shattered life, that believer's hopes can be brightened. It's the nature of things that catch light: the color and dazzle of light sparkles best through things that are shattered."[14]

Looking back at what God has done in my life reminds me of a tunnel in Switzerland. I had the opportunity to travel through this tunnel while studying French in Europe years ago. While there, I was encouraged to go to Italy to visit the friends of some colleagues. You must travel through several tunnels to get from Switzerland to Italy by train. One of those tunnels is exceptionally long. The first time I went through the tunnel,

I had no idea it was coming or how long it was. Inside the tunnel, there was total darkness.

As the train entered the heart of the mountain, it began to slow down for what seemed like an eternity. When this first happened, I became a little anxious. Why was the train going so slow? Were we going to get stuck in here? How long would this last? I turned and asked another passenger, who explained why the train may take more than 30 minutes to get through the tunnel. In the heart of the mountain, where oxygen was scarce, the engines had to slow in order not to overheat. In this tunnel, I felt the weight of the air get heavier, and breathing became more difficult as my lungs were deprived of oxygen.

Eventually, the train emerged on the other side of the mountain into the bright sunlight, fresh air, and rolling hills of northern Italy. This tunnel was long, dark, difficult, and sometimes frightening, but there was no way to get to the other side of the mountain without going through it. As we emerged from the tunnel, the light of day seemed so much brighter, the air so much fresher, and the rolling hills were a sight for sore eyes. Everything was more inviting and so much more appreciated.

This tunnel is like my journey. Your journey. Let me remind you that there's no way to get to the bright light, the fresh air, and the rolling hills except to go through the tunnel. The journey through the tunnel is necessary. Once in the tunnel, there's no turning back. You can only move forward. And going through the tunnel can give perspective. Once you are on the other side of the tunnel, you realize how wonderful the brightness of the sun, the freshness of the air, and the beauty of the hills are. You can see that the journey was worth it.

What about you? What dark tunnel are you going through? Can you see that the tunnel is part of your journey? Do you know there is light, warmth, sunshine, and rolling hills at the end of that tunnel? So don't get distracted by the darkness all around. Don't get discouraged by the length of the journey. Don't give in to despair as you struggle to breathe. And know that the journey is necessary to get to the other side. Also, know that you are not alone. He is with you. And he has sent traveling companions along to take the journey with you, to set you back on course, and remind you of your final destination.

Your trials are necessary to become the person God is shaping you to be. God is always doing something bigger than you can see or understand. James, the brother of Jesus, reminds us:

"Consider it pure joy, my brothers and sisters, whenever you face trials of many kinds, because you know that the testing of your faith produces perseverance. Let perseverance finish its work so that you may be mature and complete, not lacking anything."[15]

God just might be raising the bar for you or testing your faith. You may have fallen, but he calls you to get back up. You may have been through fire, but he calls you to keep on moving. You may have stumbled and made mistakes, but God is asking you to return to him and call on his name. He won't force you. He could easily wave his hand and make everyone follow him, but he doesn't. He gives us free will. A choice. He wants followers who choose to follow him.

You may ask why God doesn't reach down and fix this broken world. Well, my friend, the good news is that he has already begun to do just that. He sent Jesus to atone for the sins of the world, to pay the penalty, and to conquer death once and for all. And God is orchestrating his plan and molding his people in this generation like never before. The world is becoming more evil than ever, and God is raising up warriors who will stand against evil and proclaim his name. God has set you apart in this life for his purposes. The gifting God has put inside you and the trials he has taken you through are his perfect gifts. God wants to teach you to master them for his glory, not your own. He wants to use you to be "Jesus with skin on" to a lost and hurting world.

A battle has been raging since the beginning of Creation, and the enemy will lose. God calls you to be a part of his unfolding plan to win back his Creation to himself. He does not want you to be distracted by the cares and concerns of this life; he does not want you to hold anything as an idol above him. He wants you to set your sights on heaven and be used by him. The day is coming, and Jesus will return. When he does, whose side will you be on? Will you be ready?

Chapter Twenty-Five

REST

"We all wait in life for things to get easier...It will never get easier. What happens is you handle hard better...." Kara Lawson[1]

A s of the writing of this book, it has been 14 years since we left Africa. We now live on a small farm down a remote country gravel road in Missouri, almost an hour from the city, far off the beaten path. From this small piece of earth, we have carved out a refuge and a place to call home. Every once in a while, little things take me back to the good memories of Africa. A cool evening breeze. The crow of a rooster on our farm. The bleating of our goats. The smell of burning trash or wood. The beam of a flashlight in the dark.

Walking down the gravel road to our farm while the sun sets, I am reminded of the dust of Africa on my sandals as I traveled down a familiar village path not so long ago. I can almost smell the dusty air of dry season in Africa or the aroma of the cooking fires. I can almost hear the women's voices greeting me as I pass by. I envision women wrapped in their colorful panyas, their heads wrapped in cloth, balancing a load of wood or a jug of water on their heads so gracefully.

A monarch butterfly floats by in the evening sun. As I walk up to the house, the sky full and clear, I am overcome with emotion and gratitude. I am filled with a sense of God's amazing love for me. I am flawed yet redeemed. My soul is restored, and I have made peace with my trauma. I can see how he is slowly creating in me a contagious calm. And he has restored my passion for serving him. He has placed a fire inside of me that cannot be quenched. I can feel his presence with me now on this new path. Looking back, I can now see he was always walking with me.

God has graciously given us a place of therapeutic respite and healing for me and many others we have hosted over the years. But it also serves as a staging ground for what lies ahead. God has equipped us with the armor to fight the battles that remain. Now I have a battle plan. Now I am ready. The future is uncertain, yet I know my eternal future *is* certain. Many more trials still lay ahead, that much is sure, but I know that I have nothing to fear. I hear the words of Jesus spoken so long ago, yet whispered to me in a still, small voice, "*I have told you these things, so that in me you may have peace. In this world you will have trouble. But take heart! I have overcome the world.*"[2] I can trust that he is walking with me and will provide for me in the moment. My hope is in Jesus, who has prepared a place for me for all eternity. There he promises he will wipe every tear from our eyes; there will be no more death, or mourning or crying or pain, and the old order of things will have passed away.[3]

EPILOGUE

There are 7,388 known languages in the world.[1] Of those, around 1,600 are still Bibleless.[2] Today, the Forum of Bible Agencies, an alliance of 40 leading international Bible Agencies and other missions organizations, is collaborating to fulfill their shared vision of completing the task of translating the Bible into the remaining languages of the world and maximizing the access and impact of God's word.[3]

Bible.is is a new free bible app available for smartphones and computers which offers the Bible in written, oral, and dramatized format in over 1,800 languages and counting. Each year a hundred or more translations are added.[4] The New Testament translation we helped complete during our time in Africa is now among them. With a simple click, people anywhere in the world can now access God's Word in a language they can understand. It costs nothing to access the app. But what may seem like a simple app at first glance is nothing short of a miracle.

The average Bible translation can be 30+ years in the making. That's a lot of man-hours. Recording and dramatizing all of these translations required even more investment, more personnel, and more time. All of this over decades, even centuries, because everyone involved shared the same vision – to bring the Good News of God's redemptive plan to men and women of every race and to reach literally every corner of the earth. The app is no small thing.

Every one of those translations costs nearly 1 million dollars to become a reality, mainly from the generosity of millions of Christians aligning their vision with God's vision and donating funds to make it possible. But the cost cannot simply be measured in dollars. Throughout history, thousands of missionaries have followed the command of Jesus in the Great Commission recorded in the book of Matthew to "*Go and make disciples of all nations.*" [5] In the "going," countless individuals sacrificed their families, their health, and, yes, sometimes even their lives.

The obstacles faced by missionaries in the distant past were staggering. Stories of missionaries dying months after arriving in mosquito-infested jungles abound. With modern medicine and travel, the "going" may be easier, but the challenges remain, and the ultimate sacrifice is still being paid. Indeed, just a few months before the writing of this chapter, another missionary colleague lost her life unexpectedly from illness while serving on the same field we did. The instability and lack of predictability of life on the field cannot be understated.

Life overseas certainly takes its toll on the individual, not the least of which is the emotional impact of trauma. Missionaries are experiencing trauma at an alarming rate: robberies, assault, rape, murder of a friend, living through natural disasters, evacuation, loss of a child or spouse, sexual abuse, and guerrilla warfare, to name a few. [6]

But although trauma can be a big, terrifying event, it can also be a series of smaller events that can lead to the same result in the brain. Trauma occurs when an event or a series of events causes a person to lose their sense of order, justice, self-value, or a combination of these three, leading to lasting adverse effects. And although many people may go through the same trauma, not everyone may be traumatized. [7]

Immediately following a traumatic event, a person is the most vulnerable. After trauma, the person often focuses on getting to a place of safety. Any person in crisis will experience a normal, temporary state of disorganization and confusion. Many will have the resources to adjust to the situation and return to their former level of functioning. This process is more likely to go smoothly with support and crisis intervention. However, approximately 20-30% of those who experience a traumatic event will develop more severe symptoms. They may experience memory lapses, brain fog, fear, shame, insomnia, poor appetite, hopelessness, panic attacks, and loneliness.[8] The Antares Foundation suggests that around 30% of aid workers report significant symptoms of PTSD upon returning from assignment.[9]

Trauma can affect the body by getting "stuck" in the body's nervous system, impacting both voluntary and involuntary responses. Trauma can also affect one's thinking process, clouding one's perception of God, others, and self. It can alter your perception of the truth, cause you to question your faith, isolate you from others, and trigger unhealthy coping mechanisms such as alcoholism, anorexia, and cutting.[10] Trauma, especially the more severe and extended it is, can affect cognition in different ways. The individual can lose perspective and experience mental exhaustion and brain fog. If left untreated, this type of trauma can progress to varying degrees of cognitive issues and ill health.[11]

When a person has been exposed to a traumatic stressor, has re-experienced the trauma, has persistent symptoms of increased arousal for more than a month, and has exhibited avoidance behaviors, they are diagnosed with PTSD. Examples of increased arousal often include hypervigilance, exaggerated startle response, difficulty falling or staying asleep, outbursts of anger, irritability, or physiologic reactions at the exposure to situations that resemble the traumatic event.

Several secondary symptoms may also be associated with PTSD. These include depression, sadness, suicidal thoughts, poor appetite, fear of death, increased anxiety, impulsive behavior, change in lifestyle, substance abuse, and psychosomatic complaints.[12]

Another type of trauma overseas workers often experience is *moral injury*. Moral injury occurs when events unfold that go against an individual's moral beliefs or values, or upon seeing something that should be changed when nothing can be done.[13] Many of our colleagues, like us, were constantly disheartened at seeing beggars, masses of disfigured people, and people dying needlessly when Western medicine could have saved them. Overseas workers must often work in countries where corruption and injustice abound. Sometimes a person is forced to do something that goes against what they believe, such as having to pay a bribe, or a soldier having to kill another person in war. The Trauma Healing Institute calls this a *soul wound*.[14]

Another type of trauma is *survivor's guilt*. This happens when a person feels guilt because they survived when others did not. This is an experience common to cancer survivors, war veterans, and even missionaries.[15]

Cumulative grief, cumulative/complex trauma, or *cumulative stress* occurs when a person has not processed one loss, trauma, or stressor before another takes place.[16] For missionaries, cumulative trauma combined with cumulative stress is all too common. Missionaries can also experience complex trauma when they go to their fields of service, having already experienced childhood trauma, such as physical, sexual, or emotional abuse, which may never have been addressed or resolved. They may be able to function well for many years, but often the increasingly stressful environment of the mission field brings out symptoms of their unresolved trauma that can no longer be ignored.[17]

Secondary trauma is experienced when one witnesses, assists with, or hears about someone else's trauma, such as a close friend, co-worker, or national.[18] Because missionaries tend to work in close community with their colleagues, secondary trauma is common. Secondary trauma can also have a more significant impact when combined with one's own trauma or complex trauma experiences, or when it triggers PTSD.

Most missionaries are quality individuals with years of often highly specialized training. They are generally adventurous, strong, courageous, sacrificial, and dedicated, with a strong sense of "calling." Many, like me, first leave for their assigned field full of enthusiasm and hope. Mission agencies often require months, even years, of rigorous training to prepare their members for the stress, transition, and challenges that lie ahead. But expecting stress and change is one thing; encountering it is another. These same strong individuals too often leave the field traumatized, defeated, broken, disillusioned, and even bitter. Additionally, statistics show that about 46% of missionaries will leave their field of service with a mood or mental disorder due to their ministry, and 87% of those include depression.[19] This is particularly common among those who lack adequate social support.[20]

Over the past several years, I have interviewed missionaries I knew personally and collected parts of their stories of how they experienced fear, trauma, stress, and crisis. Many of them have faced overwhelming obstacles and still serve on their respective fields today. Others have left their fields of service for various reasons, including the inability to cope with stress or devastating trauma. Among some of the more intense traumatic experiences these missionaries endured were evacuations, terrorist attacks, losing homes in fires, cyclones, rioting and civil unrest, food and fuel shortages, gunfire, the murder of a national colleague, vehicle accidents, evacuating a child who was critically ill or injured, rape, death of a spouse on the field, bombings, and witnessing mass deaths or massacres.

A recurring theme of trauma and stress that many missionaries mentioned in my interviews involved epidemics, the most recent ones being Ebola and COVID-19. One recollected how they struggled with a constant fear of death during the Ebola epidemic in West Africa. One individual mentioned the stress of hearing wailing from neighbors grieving the loss of a loved one, or dealing with the moral injury of African neighbors who were ostracized or abandoned because they had become ill with the virus and were left to die. COVID lockdowns left several families I interviewed stranded and isolated on their fields, sometimes for years, unable to leave or return to their home country. One family almost lost a child during lockdowns as they could not get him adequate medical care. Those working in medical mission work reported struggling with the ongoing trauma of dealing with difficult medical cases without the support and infrastructure offered by more developed countries. And similar to my own experiences treating patients in Africa, witnessing overwhelming suffering and death on an ongoing basis without the resources to intervene caused moral injury for many I interviewed.

But aside from these more intense traumatic circumstances, there were also cases of missionaries experiencing trauma responses, such as PTSD, yet they could not point out a single traumatic event. This is because a series of smaller events can lead to the same result in the brain.[21] A myriad of other stressors can cause instability and emotional turmoil in the lives of missionaries and other overseas workers.

Missionaries are human like anyone else and will instinctually have human reactions to things around them, even with the best intentions and training, and even when they are relatively mature spiritually. People generally become more distressed when faced with instability and even more so when it threatens their identity, culture, environment, safety, and social support systems. The more transitions and unexpected changes a person experiences, the more distress he feels. When layer after layer of unstable scenarios are placed on an already shaky framework, it is no wonder that people are pushed into emotional crises.[22]

Common trauma-causing struggles for most missionaries include sickness and dealing with healthcare systems in other countries. Many illnesses or injuries require medical evacuation due to the lack of adequate care in host countries. Many missionaries mentioned having secondary trauma, having to walk through trauma, death, medical crises, or evacuations with colleagues or nationals. Common themes I heard from those I interviewed were inadequate medical care, incompetency of healthcare workers, unfamiliar ways of doing things, lack of needed medicines, the need to drive around to multiple locations to get needed care, and lack of empathy and concern on the part of medical staff.

One family shared how, when their daughter's arm was broken, the hospital staff didn't care that they were hurting her and ended up not setting the arm properly. Events like this caused this family to question their decision to serve in their host country. They often faced guilt about endangering their family unnecessarily. They dealt with criticism from colleagues, family, and supporters back home on how they handled their child's health emergency. The result was their daughter living with a lifelong deformity.

A myriad of other stressors experienced in overseas work can impact an individual's physical and mental health. The stress of interacting with authorities in the host country was also a common theme mentioned by those I interviewed. Some missionaries shared how they had to report to authorities in their host country and have their activity scrutinized. They lived in constant fear of being held for questioning or getting kicked out of the country. One woman shared how her heart would start racing every time there was an unexpected knock on the door.

Logistic challenges in the host country were another common source of stress. Individuals reported how things that seemed so simple — like driving, grocery shopping, paying bills, or sleeping — suddenly became extraordinarily challenging and stressful. One person said driving in the capital city of their host country was a constant source of anxiety.

Many shared that they didn't realize what weight they were carrying from all the stress until they left the country for a home assignment. Several missionaries shared how they needed breaks, but sometimes getting to and from vacations was so stressful they would avoid vacations altogether. One individual said driving back to their home in the city after a vacation undid all the rest that the holiday accomplished.

In surveys conducted by many organizations, the number one reason given by missionaries for leaving the field is interper-

sonal conflict.[23] Because of this, modern mission agencies pour countless resources into training their members in conflict resolution. Despite
this, conflicts remain among the most difficult challenges cross-cultural
workers face. Conflicts often center around unmet expectations, especially for younger individuals who idealize their roles and what they hope
to accomplish. Jealousy can also creep into relationships because humans
are, by nature, sinful creatures.[24] Other causes of conflict that emerged
in surveys included personality issues, manipulation, criticism, division,
integrity issues, and pride.[25]

With individuals I interviewed, conflict between teammates was a
common theme. Examples were conflicting opinions about how things
were done, moral issues, conflicts with national workers, failure to meet
the expectations of others, and having to be "fake" to keep the peace.
One individual shared how difficult it was to keep team personnel on
the same page, as people often changed their minds. One shared how she
didn't feel supported by her mission leadership.

One woman shared how conflict with an African worker caused her
to become depressed and shut down emotionally. Daily stresses added to
the depression, and she became introverted. The patterns of depression
linger to this day years later. This individual has had to unlearn a lifelong
pattern of stuffing emotions.

Several people recounted how they struggled with feeling inadequate,
wondering if they were doing enough in ministry and living up to the
perceived expectations of others. Conflicting expectations from both
co-workers and nationals were common. Disputes arose over living too
affluently or roughing it too much. Several missionaries mentioned feeling isolated and lonely, even around nationals and their teammates. This
was common for both single and married individuals.

Another common team issue was the grief felt at losing other teammates. Individuals felt abandoned, isolated, and forced to carry the burden alone when team members left the field. Sometimes the loss of

teammates meant the loss of a shared dream or even the inability to do a job because it depended on the presence of the ones who left. One expressed their grief of losing colleagues and co-workers who had become family, their church family, and their emotional support. Some described how stressful it was to close out the homes of families who had left and get rid of their belongings. Several missionaries in administrative roles recounted how they had to do this with multiple families in a short period of time. One couple had to do this for seven families simultaneously due to families fleeing the country at the beginning of the COVID-19 epidemic. Upon learning that co-workers weren't returning, this missionary described how she developed panic attacks.

An all-too-frequent stressor involved finances and supporting churches. Many individuals reported that communicating with supporters, raising support, and keeping up appearances was a significant strain. Several related a constant struggle to live up to the expectations of their supporting churches. The fact that stress often caused the person to question his or her calling or feel like a failure was also repeatedly shared. It is unsurprising that many missionaries fear telling their supporting churches about their struggles on the field.

Several missionaries mentioned they had conflicts in their marriages. In some cases, the marriage dysfunctions were present under the surface but were amplified after going to the field of service. In others, the stress of living cross-culturally created conflicts that were not already present.

Having to deal with ailing parents was another theme. Multiple individuals told of how one or both parents died while they were overseas. The logistics of getting a flight out or finding the finances to do so were often prohibitive. They shared how they grieved missed opportunities, missed memories, and how it was hard to have closure.

A very common struggle missionaries reported was with their children. The challenges faced by children of missionaries and overseas workers, also known as Third Culture Kids (TCKs), have gained much attention in the past several decades. Families struggled with fear for their children's safety, physical and mental health, or going through puberty in the host culture. Several explained that while Africa might be a young boy's paradise, it often leaves teen girls feeling isolated in cultures where their same-age peers are getting married and having babies.

Sexual abuse by nationals and even other missionary children was an issue dealt with by many. In some cases, families felt pressure to allow their children to interact freely with national children to adapt to the culture and language, only to discover their child was abused. These same individuals also struggled with guilt for exposing their children to missionary life. Some TCKs developed mental health issues because of it. Some families regretted robbing their kids of a "normal" childhood in the home country or time with grandparents. This parental guilt was a common reason people cited for questioning if they were following God's will or not.

A related issue was dealing with adult TCKs who grow up and have trouble adjusting to their home culture. Many families reported children leaving their faith or resenting parents for taking them overseas, leaving them at boarding school, or leaving them in their home country to navigate life alone after graduating high school.

The struggle to know God's will was a recurring theme. One person shared how overwhelming it was to hear dozens of conflicting opinions from others about how they should interpret God's will in a given situation. She reported shutting down, being sad often, and sometimes getting angry. She described how easy it was to get stuck in unhealthy thought patterns and give in to anxiety. Many said they wish they had dealt more thoroughly with issues from their past before going to the field, as those matters compounded their problems on the field.

An overwhelming number of people I spoke to recounted how they or their children experienced permanent changes in health from either stress or illnesses, often developing health issues that required them to leave the field. These included asthma, thyroid dysfunction, migraines, lowered immunity, gastrointestinal problems, and chronic fatigue syndrome. A majority of them shared how they or at least one family member now have some form of mental health issue that they did not struggle with before their time on the field. These included panic attacks, anxiety, insomnia, nightmares, racing thoughts, irritability, personality changes, bipolar disorder, depression, obsessive-compulsive tendencies, and PTSD.

One missionary, now working for a missionary care organization, reported how shocked she was at the high number of missionaries reporting suicidal thoughts. Additionally, of those I interviewed, several said that family members experienced mental health changes, even suicidal thoughts, after taking one of the common anti-malarial medications on a weekly basis. These side effects are now widely recognized with this medication. One believes they have permanent mental health changes from taking that medication for so many years. Many reported having to take anti-depressants, anxiety medications, or other psychotropic medications on an ongoing basis.

Many individuals reported a lack of good help for their developing mental health challenges. They described insufficient debriefing and care facilities for helping them process trauma, crisis, conflict, and overwhelming stress. Many expressed a need for in-depth care but were then referred to places that were too expensive, too far away, and offered no options for their children. Reentry care for missionaries returning to their home country permanently was also mentioned as almost non-existent in most cases. Some said they felt judged and misunderstood by others for leaving the field, and they did not feel free to share with supporters about their struggles or the suffering they endured.

In surveys reported by *The Mission Experience*,[26] the following percentage of people attributed certain factors as part of their decision to leave their field of service:

- 74% - burnout
- 70% - discouragement and anxiety in their family
- 69% - too many stressors or isolation/loneliness
- 67% - depression in the family
- 64% - frequent transitions
- 61% - difficulty setting boundaries on what was demanded of them
- 59% - traumatic experiences
- 59% - pressured to produce results
- 53% - felt overwhelmed with too much work and too little help
- 51% - felt unsafe or experienced a feeling of not belonging anywhere
- 40% - no longer felt called to the host country
- 55% - felt a new call to something in home country
- 47% - felt a disconnection in relationship with the Lord
- 47% - struggled to connect with a local church
- 46% - felt that pastors and church members back home had forgotten about them
- 38% - uncertainty if methods were effective
- 23% - unsure of their faith (or spouse was no longer sure of faith)
- 38% - no longer sure of their calling (or spouse no longer sure)
- 33% - worked themselves out of a job or were no longer needed
- 15% - moral failure by self, spouse, or child that damaged witness
- 41% - felt overwhelmed by spiritual oppression
- 44% - inadequate preparation for life on the mission field
- 38% - felt unequipped for the work they were assigned to
- 50% - felt that their job did not meet their expectations
- 58% - struggled to find meaningful community
- 45% - interpersonal dysfunction on the team
- 52% - significant health problems
- 38% - spouse that experienced significant health problems
- 33% - children that experienced significant health problems

- 60% - inadequate health care in the host country
- 50% - stress affecting the health of others in their family
- 36% - limited access to clean water
- 42% - climate or geography affecting their health negatively
- 47% - pollution affecting their health negatively

Sending churches usually believe everything is fine with the missionaries they send out because missionary newsletters are often full of exciting ministry progress. It is essential for sending churches to know that the confident, strong missionaries they send out will most likely, at some point, experience overwhelming stress or trauma. From my own experience, I have concluded that it is not a question of *if*, but rather a question of *when, how often,* and *to what extent.*

Despite the months or even years of preparation that sending agencies and churches may provide, more needs to be done by those agencies and churches to create an environment of compassion, pastoral care, and crisis intervention for battle-scarred overseas workers. Though spiritual care is a vital part of this, telling a missionary to "just pray about it" is usually not helpful. They've often heard advice like that before and have likely already done it. Being aware that something more is needed is vital.

The tragedy of trauma among overseas workers is that many of the more severe symptoms and disorders they may develop can be prevented and treated, especially if recognized early on. However, all too often, considerable damage has already been done by the time the problem is identified. Then, recovery and healing may take much longer, and the impact may be greater. In many cases, the missionary will have to leave the field for an extended period or may be unable to return.[27]

Crisis debriefing, or critical incident stress debriefing, is a service more and more overseas organizations are providing. According to experts, crisis debriefing should ideally occur within the first 24-72 hours after a critical incident to minimize the impact of the trauma on the individual. Continual emotional support should also be provided in the hours and days following the incident.[28] I am thankful that these services began to be implemented in my latter years on the field. Whole member care organizations have now been formed both nationally and internationally to assist with this much-needed ministry.

Additionally, leadership in organizations should be trained and equipped to recognize the early signs of stress or mental illness in their members so that early interventions can be provided. Those who experience multiple and prolonged symptoms of stress-related disorders should be referred to a mental health professional.[29] Therapeutic parish communities and support groups are also needed.[30] Finally, supporting churches must cultivate pastoral and compassionate relationships with their missionaries that promote healing and resilience.

Tips for Trauma Recovery

Listing tips may appear to be a simple way to address something as complex as trauma. I am by no means making light of the incredible struggle many face in dealing with their trauma. An essential fact to understand is that healing from trauma is not a one-and-done deal. Instead, it is a linear process and takes time. Some days will be easy, but triggers may bring the trauma back on other days. Allowances should be made for these ups and downs.[31]

Shonna Ingram offers some practical suggestions for starters in her article, *How to start healing from trauma.*[32] Here are those steps in a nutshell:

1. Get out of the crisis.
2. Pay attention not only to the things you are saying but also to how you are reacting to things.
3. Become familiar with the stages of grief: denial, anger, bargaining, depression, and acceptance.
4. Find safe places where stories, emotions, and feelings can be shared without judgment.
5. Reach out to a professional counselor, trauma coach, or trauma-

informed spiritual leader.

6. Consider effective trauma treatment modalities such as EMDR, Brainspotting, Internal Family Systems, Emotional Freedom Techniques, tapping, Somatic Therapy, or Healing Prayer.

7. Become involved in a trauma-informed community, such as Renewed Hope Approach.

8. Helping others.

For a more in-depth discussion of these topics, please consult the reference section at the end of this book.

ADDITIONAL RESOURCES

Eldredge, J. (2022). *Resilient: Restoring Your Weary Soul in These Turbulent Times.* Thomas Nelson.

Firestone, L. (2012). *Recognizing Complex Trauma. Psychology Today.*

Ingram, S. (2021a). *Your Path of Renewed Hope: Clarify Your Next Steps, Workbook 1: Restore foundation.* Amazon.

Ingram, S. (2021b). *Your Path of Renewed Hope: Clarify Your Next Steps, Workbook 2: Receive foundation.* Amazon.

Ingram, S. (2021c). *Your Path of Renewed Hope: Clarify Your Next Steps, Workbook 3: Rebuild foundation.* Amazon.

Kübler-Ross, E. (2003). *On Death and Dying.* Simon and Schuster.

Langberg, D. (2015). *Suffering and the Heart of God: How Trauma Destroys and Christ Restores.* New Growth Press.

Schaefer, F.C., & Schaefer, C.A. (2022). *Trauma & Resilience: A Handbook.*

Story, L. (2015). *When God Doesn't Fix It: Lessons You Never Wanted to Learn; Truths You Can't Live Without.* W. Publishing.

Thompson, C. (2010). *Anatomy of the Soul: Surprising Connections between Neuroscience and Spiritual Practices That Can Transform Your Life and Relationships.* Tyndale House.

Trauma Healing Institute. (2023). *Beyond Disaster: A Survivor's Guide for Spiritual First Aid.*

Van der Kolk, B. (2015). *The Body Keeps the Score: Brain, Mind, and Body in the Healing of Trauma.* Penguin Books.

Wright, H. N. (2016). *When the Past Won't Let You Go: Find the Healing That Helps You Move On.* Harvest House Publishers.

REFERENCES

Introduction
1. Escalante, A. (2019). U.S. leads in the worldwide anxiety epidemic. *Psychology Today, April 26, 2019.* https://www.psychologytoday.com/us/blog/shouldstorm/201904/us-leads-in-the-worldwide-anxiety-epidemic
2. Bethune, S. (2019). Gen Z more likely to report mental health concerns. *American Psychological Association, 50*(1), p. 20. https://www.apa.org/monitor/2019/01/gen-z
3. Richter, S (2008). *The epic of eden.* IVP Academic

Chapter 1
1. Elliot, E. (1957). *Through gates of splendor.* New York: Harper & Brothers.

Chapter 2
1. Psalm 23:4, New International Version.

Chapter 3
1. Crabb, L. (2013). *Inside out.* Nav Press.

Chapter 4
1. 2 Corinthians 12:7

Chapter 5
1. 1 John 4:4

Chapter 6
1. Friedman, M. (2022). PTSD history and overview. https://www.ptsd.va.gov/professional/treat/essentials/history_ptsd.asp

Chapter 12
1. Lucado, M. (2017). *Anxious for nothing.* Thomas Nelson.
2. Philippians 4:5-6

Chapter 13
1. Galatians 6:9. New International Version.
2. Ephesians 6:13. New International Version.

Chapter 16
1. Mark 11:23-24. New International Version.
2. Job 1:20
3. Herms, B. & Hall, J.M. (2005). Praise You In This Storm [Recorded by Casting Crowns]. On *Lifesong* [CD]. Be Essential Songs (BMI) / My Refuge Music (BMI).

Chapter 17
1. Psalm 30:5b. New International Version.
2. Psalm 9:1-5. New International Version.
3. Psalm 10:17-18. New International Version.
4. Psalm 13:1-2a, 3, 5-6. New International Version.
5. Philippians 4:6-7. New International Version.
6. Psalm 51:12, New International Version.
7. 1 Thessalonians 3:3, New International Version.
8. The Tertullian Project. (2021). https://www.tertullian.org

Chapter 18
1. Psalm 91:4, New Living Translation.

Chapter 19
1. Psalm 23:4, New International Version.

Chapter 21
1. Palmer, P. (2000), p. 4-5. *Let your life speak.* Jossey-Bass Inc.
2. Curtis, B. & Eldridge, J. (1997). The sacred romance: Drawing closer to the heart of God. Thomas Nelson.
3. Buechner, F. (1992). *Telling secrets.* Harperone.
4. Jeremiah, D. (2000), p. 57. *When your world falls apart.* Word Publishing.
5. Friesen, G. & Maxson, R. (2004). *Decision making and the will of God.* Multnomah.
6. Job 2:9, New International Version.
7. Job 1:21, New International Version.
8. John 6:68, New International Version.
9. Matthew 16:24
10. Mother Theresa. https://www.catholic.org/clife/teresa/quotes.php
11. Matthew 10:11-13
12. Romans 12:3-8
13. Mark 4:26-29
14. James 1:17a, New Living Translation.

Chapter 23
1. Tolkien, J. R. R. (1955). *The return of the king.* Macmillan.
2. Matthew 14:22-36, New International Version.

3. Psalm 23:4, New International Version.
4. Psalm 23:5, New International Version.
5. Hebrews 13:5-6, New International Version.
6. Psalm 27:1-3, New International Version.
7. Ephesians 6:12, New International Version.
8. 2 Corinthians 2:11, New International Version.
9. 1 Peter 5:8, New International Version.
10. John 8:44, New International Version.
11. Romans 12:2, New International Version.
12. Ephesians 6:10-20

Chapter 24
1. Romans 8:28, New International Version.
2. James 1:2-4
3. Jeremiah 29:11
4. Jeremiah 18
5. Isaiah 45:9
6. Numbers 22
7. John 9:2-3, New International Version.
8. John 11:4, New International Version.
9. Acts 7-9
10. Acts 8
11. Genesis 45:8, New International Version.
12. Genesis 50:20, New International Version.
13. 2 Corinthians 12:7, New International Version.
14. Erickson, J. (2010), May 8. *Diamonds in the dust.* Zondervan.
15. James 1:2-4, New International Version.

Chapter 25
1. Lawson, K. https://thespun.com/more/top-stories/look-message-from-dukes-kara-lawson-is-going-viral
2. John 16:33, New International Version.
3. Revelation 21:4

Epilogue
1. Wycliffe Global Alliance. (2023). 2022 Global Scripture Access. https://www.wycliffe.net/resources/statistics/
2. Pioneer Bible Translators. (2023). https://pioneerbible.org/
3. Forum of Bible Agencies. (2023). About Us. https://forum-intl.org/about/
4. Faith Comes by Hearing. *Bible.is.* https://www.faithcomesbyhearing.com/audio-bible-resources/bible-is
5. Matthew 28:19, New International Version.
6. Carr, K. (2015). Trauma and post-traumatic stress disorder among missionaries: How to recognize, prevent, and treat it. *Missio Nexus.* Retrieved from https://missionexus.org/trauma-and-post-traumatic-stress-disorder-among-missionaries-how-to-recognize-prevent-and-treat-it/

7. Ingram, S. (2023). The unseen trauma of the mission field: What trauma is and what it does. *A Life Overseas.* Retrieved from https://www.alifeoverseas.com/the-unseen-trauma-of-the-mission-field-what-trauma-is-and-what-it-does/

8. Carr, K. (2015). Trauma and post-traumatic stress disorder among missionaries: How to recognize, prevent, and treat it. *Missio Nexus.* Retrieved from https://missionexus.org/trauma-and-post-traumatic-stress-disorder-among-missionaries-how-to-recognize-prevent-and-treat-it/

9. McEachran, R. (2014). Aid workers and post-traumatic stress disorder. *The Guardian.* Retrieved from https://www.theguardian.com/global-development-professionals-network/2014/mar/03/post-traumantic-stress-disorder-aid-workers/

10. Ingram, S. (2023). The unseen trauma of the mission field: What trauma is and what it does. *A Life Overseas.* Retrieved from https://www.alifeoverseas.com/the-unseen-trauma-of-the-mission-field-what-trauma-is-and-what-it-does/

11. Casteneda, R. (2021). How major traumatic events can impact your long-term health. *U.S. News and World Report,* Sept. 21. Retrieved from https://health.usnews.com/wellness/articles/how-major-traumatic-events-can-impact-your-long-term-health/

12. Carr, K. (2015). Trauma and post-traumatic stress disorder among missionaries: How to recognize, prevent, and treat it. *Missio Nexus.* Retrieved from https://missionexus.org/trauma-and-post-traumatic-stress-disorder-among-missionaries-how-to-recognize-prevent-and-treat-it/

13. Ingram, S. (2023). How trauma shows up on the field: The unseen trauma on the mission field part 2. *A Life Overseas.* Retrieved from https://www.alifeoverseas.com/how-trauma-shows-up-on-the-field-the-unseen-trauma-of-the-mission-field-part-2/

14. Trauma Healing Institute. https://www.traumahealinginstitute.org/

15. Ingram, S. (2023). How trauma shows up on the field: The unseen trauma on the mission field part 2. *A Life Overseas.* Retrieved from https://www.alifeoverseas.com/how-trauma-shows-up-on-the-field-the-unseen-trauma-of-the-mission-field-part-2/

16. Ingram, S. (2023). How trauma shows up on the field: The unseen trauma on the mission field part 2. *A Life Overseas.* Retrieved from https://www.alifeoverseas.com/how-trauma-shows-up-on-the-field-the-unseen-trauma-of-the-mission-field-part-2/

17. Carr, K. (2015). Trauma and post-traumatic stress disorder among missionaries: How to recognize, prevent, and treat it. *Missio Nexus*. Retrieved from https://missionexus.org/trauma-and-post-traumatic-stress-disorder-among-missionaries-how-to-recognize-prevent-and-treat-it/

18. Carr, K. (2015). Trauma and post-traumatic stress disorder among missionaries: How to recognize, prevent, and treat it. *Missio Nexus*. Retrieved from https://missionexus.org/trauma-and-post-traumatic-stress-disorder-among-missionaries-how-to-recognize-prevent-and-treat-it/

19. Free Rain International. https://www.freerainint.org/

20. Casteneda, R. (2021). How major traumatic events can impact your long-term health. *U.S. News and World Report, Sept. 21.* https://health.usnews.com/wellness/articles/how-major-traumatic-events-can-impact-your-long-term-health/

21. Ingram, S. (2023). The unseen trauma of the mission field: What trauma is and what it does. *A Life Overseas.* https://www.alifeoverseas.com/the-unseen-trauma-of-the-mission-field-what-trauma-is-and-what-it-does/

22. The Mission Experience. (2023). Missionary attrition survey: Stressors and mental health factors. *The Mission Experience.* https://themissionexperience.weebly.com/

23. Akin, P. (2017). The number one reason missionaries leave the field. *Baptist Press.* https://www.baptistpress.com/resource-library/news/the-number-one-reason-missionaries-leave-the-field/

24. Akin, P. (2017). The number one reason missionaries leave the field. *Baptist Press.* https://www.baptistpress.com/resource-library/news/the-number-one-reason-missionaries-leave-the-field/

25. The Mission Experience. (2023). Missionary attrition survey: Stressors and mental health factors. *The Mission Experience.* https://themissionexperience.weebly.com/

26. The Mission Experience. (2023). Missionary attrition survey: Stressors and mental health factors. *The Mission Experience.* https://themissionexperience.weebly.com/

27. Carr, K. (2015). Trauma and post-traumatic stress disorder among missionaries: How to recognize, prevent, and treat it. *Missio Nexus*. Retrieved from https://missionexus.org/trauma-and-post-traumatic-stress-disorder-among-missionaries-how-to-recognize-prevent-and-treat-it/

28. Carr, K. (2015). Trauma and post-traumatic stress disorder among missionaries: How to recognize, prevent, and treat it. *Missio Nexus.* Retrieved from https://missionexus.org/trauma-and-post-traumatic-stress-disorder-among-missionaries-how-to-recognize-prevent-and-treat-it/

29. Carr, K. (1994). Trauma and post-traumatic stress disorder among missionaries. *Mobile Member Care Team.* https://www.ywammembercare.net/uploads/1/3/0/9/130964492/trauma_and_post-traumatic_stress_disorder_among_missionaries.pdf

30. Sinclair, N. J. R. (1993). *Horrific traumata: A pastoral response to the post-traumatic stress disorder.* New York: Routledge.

31. Ingram, S. (2023). How to start healing from trauma: The unseen trauma of the mission field part 3. *A Life Overseas.* https://www.alifeoverseas.com/how-to-start-healing-from-trauma-the-unseen-trauma-of-the-mission-field-part-3/

32. Ingram, S. (2023). How to start healing from trauma: The unseen trauma of the mission field part 3. *A Life Overseas.* https://www.alifeoverseas.com/how-to-start-healing-from-trauma-the-unseen-trauma-of-the-mission-field-part-3/